Cambridge Elements

Elements in American Politics
edited by
Frances E. Lee
Princeton University

THE POLITICAL DYNAMICS OF PARTISAN POLARIZATION

Eric R. Schmidt
Millsaps College

Edward G. Carmines
Indiana University

Paul M. Sniderman
Stanford University

Shaftesbury Road, Cambridge CB2 8EA, United Kingdom

One Liberty Plaza, 20th Floor, New York, NY 10006, USA

477 Williamstown Road, Port Melbourne, VIC 3207, Australia

314–321, 3rd Floor, Plot 3, Splendor Forum, Jasola District Centre, New Delhi – 110025, India

103 Penang Road, #05–06/07, Visioncrest Commercial, Singapore 238467

Cambridge University Press is part of Cambridge University Press & Assessment, a department of the University of Cambridge.

We share the University's mission to contribute to society through the pursuit of education, learning and research at the highest international levels of excellence.

www.cambridge.org
Information on this title: www.cambridge.org/9781009472791
DOI: 10.1017/9781009472760

© Eric R. Schmidt, Edward G. Carmines and Paul M. Sniderman 2025

This publication is in copyright. Subject to statutory exception and to the provisions of relevant collective licensing agreements, no reproduction of any part may take place without the written permission of Cambridge University Press & Assessment.

When citing this work, please include a reference to the DOI 10.1017/9781009472760

First published 2025

A catalogue record for this publication is available from the British Library

ISBN 978-1-009-47279-1 Hardback
ISBN 978-1-009-47278-4 Paperback
ISSN 2515-1606 (online)
ISSN 2515-1592 (print)

Additional resources for this publication at www.cambridge.org/schmidt

Cambridge University Press & Assessment has no responsibility for the persistence or accuracy of URLs for external or third-party internet websites referred to in this publication and does not guarantee that any content on such websites is, or will remain, accurate or appropriate.

The Political Dynamics of Partisan Polarization

Elements in American Politics

DOI: 10.1017/9781009472760
First published online: February 2025

Eric R. Schmidt
Millsaps College

Edward G. Carmines
Indiana University

Paul M. Sniderman
Stanford University

Author for correspondence: Eric R. Schmidt, schmier@millsaps.edu

Abstract: This is a study of the dynamics of partisan polarization in the United States. It has three objectives: (1) to identify and explain why some Republicans and Democrats – but not others – have polarized, particularly over the last twenty years; (2) to demonstrate that they have done so not on this or that issue but systematically, programmatically – domain versus issue sorting; and (3) to bring into the open profound asymmetries in polarization between the two parties, not least that Republicans polarized early and thoroughly on issues of race, while Democrats in the largest number stayed neutral or even conservative until only recently. Emerging from the reasoning and results is a revised theory of party identification that specifies the conditions under which ordinary Republicans and Democrats can become ideological partisans – real-life conservatives and liberals in their behavior – in the choices they make on candidates, policies, and parties.

Keywords: party identification, American politics, ideology, partisan sorting, polarization

© Eric R. Schmidt, Edward G. Carmines and Paul M. Sniderman 2025

ISBNs: 9781009472791 (HB), 9781009472784 (PB), 9781009472760 (OC)
ISSNs: 2515-1606 (online), 2515-1592 (print)

Contents

1 Theory 1

2 Dynamics of Partisan Polarization 14

3 Implications 64

   References 74

1 Theory

This is a work of six hands in the service of one idea: in the study of political psychology, the political comes first. To avoid misunderstanding at the outset, we unconditionally agree that psychologically oriented analyses of mass publics have paid handsome dividends. Disciplinary arbitrage pays. But if it is politics you want to understand, you must get clear – quite clear – what you are attempting to explain before you attempt to explain it.

That, at any rate, is the controlling premise of this Element. Our objective on every page is to bring into the open the politics, not the psychology, of polarization. What are Republicans and Democrats actually disagreeing about? How deep are their disagreements? Are Republicans becoming more conservative, Democrats more liberal, or are more Republicans becoming conservative, more Democrats liberal – or both? When is polarization symmetrical, with Republicans and Democrats both lining up behind their parties' platforms? When is it asymmetrical, with one party polarizing early and thoroughly, the other lagging well behind? And, not least, what is the answer to the question that politics is ultimately about – who has the upper hand, when, and why?

1.1 The Challenge

Polarization is a chameleon concept. For some, polarization signals policy extremism, a propulsive move to the ideological poles (Abramowitz 2010, 2013, 2015; Abramowitz and Saunders 1998, 2006, 2008). For others, it is a stand-in for regular Republicans and Democrats increasingly taking their party's side on an assortment of issues – issue sorting in the academic argot (Fiorina 2017; Fiorina, Abrams, and Pope 2011; Hetherington 2009; Levendusky 2009, 2010). For still others, it flags the enlistment of regular Republicans and Democrats in the service of an overarching ideological program (Bafumi and Shapiro 2009) and, as a result, their antipathy to the opposing party (see Costa 2021; Orr and Huber 2020). And for yet others, polarization is raw emotion, a "fear and loathing" of the opposing party (Iyengar and Krupenkin 2018; Iyengar, Sood, and Lelkes 2012). Arguments can be made for each of these ways of thinking about polarization. They may not all have equal force, but they all have a claim to credibility given the evidence at hand. Hence our decision to take a different path.

1.1.1 Preamble

Our aim is to present and test a theory of the politics of polarization. The framework is institutional, narrowly circumscribed. Meso-institutions, the commingling of parties and interest groups, and the nationalization of politics are background presumptions (see Pierson and Schickler 2020, 2024). Electoral competition, through the constraints of a two-party system, is the pivotal institution, ideas in the form of policy preferences the focus. By way of warning, austerity is the objective – the minimum number of assumptions, the minimum number of constructs, and the minimum number of connections between them. Transparency, simplicity is the goal.

1.1.2 A Stylized View

Generically conceived, partisan polarization consists of supporters of the two parties adopting increasingly divergent perspectives, one liberal, the other conservative. Figure 1 presents a stylized sketch. The vertical axis maps the ideological poles; the more conservative, the closer to the top; the more liberal, the closer to the bottom; and the dashes midway between top and bottom pick out the midpoint between the two. The horizontal axis maps the period of time our account covers, 1972 through 2020. The dashed ascending line tracks the degree to which Republican identifiers become progressively more conservative; the solid descending line tracks the degree to which Democratic identifiers become progressively more liberal.

Symmetrical divergence is the stand-out feature in this stylized account of polarization. Before polarization, though Republicans tend to the conservative

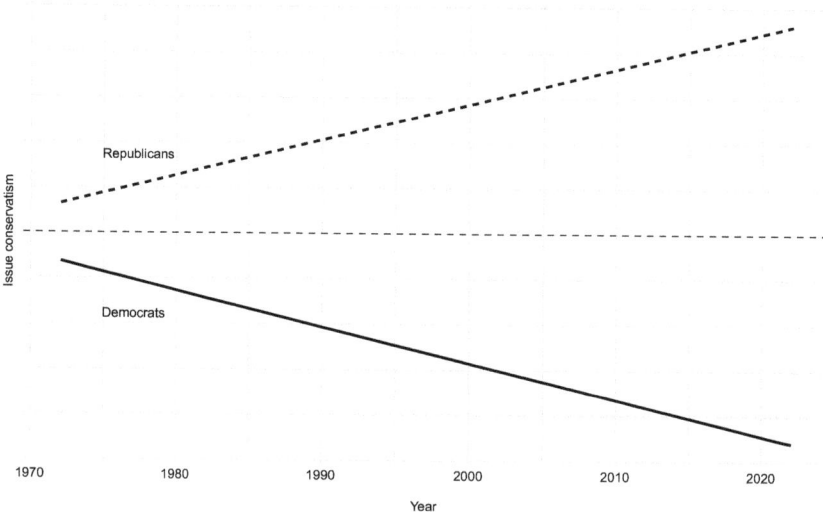

Figure 1 Symmetrical polarization: the standard narrative. The graph illustrates what mass polarization might look like if Republican and Democratic identifiers polarized at the same time and pace.

side and Democrats to the liberal side, the difference between them is narrow. As politics polarizes, the two diverge, with Republicans becoming increasingly conservative and Democrats increasingly liberal. Partisan polarization is thus symmetrical, both parties moving to their respective poles at the same time and the same rate nearly enough.

1.2 Domain Sorting

Our objective is to develop and test a theory centered on the politics of polarization. Research on mass polarization has focused on "issue sorting," with party supporters taking the side of their party on particular issues. Our concern is sorting on a larger scale – regular Republicans and Democrats siding with their party, not higgledy-piggledy on this or that issue, but systematically and programmatically. The parties-in-government's competition for electoral support recurrently centers on three policy domains: Social welfare – what is the responsibility of government to help those who are disadvantaged? Racial politics – how far and by what means should government promote racial equality? Cultural politics – what is right, what is wrong, on issues like abortion and gay rights?

In conceptualizing sorting at the level of domains rather than issues, we take advantage of Converse's (1964) concept of "natural wholes." Public intellectuals, political polemicists, and candidates make the case that the ideas that the parties stand for go together "naturally" (Noel 2013). To say "naturally" is to acknowledge, Converse remarked, that "the shaping of belief systems of any range into apparently logical wholes that are credible to large numbers of people is an act of creative synthesis" (Converse 1964, 211). Creative, because some connections are only quasi-logical or just fortuitous; synthesis, because issues in the same policy domain tend to share a common rationale. Strictly logical or not, just so far as their party's positions form a "natural whole," their supporters can take hold of them as a whole.

Under the pressure of the ideological polarization of the parties-in-government, the policy preferences of their supporters in the electorate have increasingly become organized along liberal-conservative lines (e.g., Hare 2022; Hare, Highton, and Jones 2024). However, the fact that the politics of social welfare, race, and culture have converged on a common dimension does not mean that they have followed a common trajectory. Social welfare politics, we shall show, reflects the deepening of New Deal divisions between Democrats and Republicans. By contrast, racial politics have been astonishingly one-sided until very recently. Last but not least, cultural politics is quicksilver politics, moving toward consensus on gay rights while erupting with new controversies, for example, over the rights of transgender people. Three policy agendas with three distinct trajectories. Hence our focus on domain sorting rather than issue sorting.

1.3 A Political Conception of Political Polarization

From a social-psychological perspective, partisan polarization *is* loyalty politics. Republicans follow their leaders, and Democrats follow theirs because they are emotionally attached to their party (Achen and Bartels 2016; Huddy, Mason, and Aarøe 2015; Mason 2014, 2018; Mason and Wronski 2018) – not because they share their parties' ideological or programmatic commitments in any significant sense.

Our concern is regular Republicans and Democrats. It is agreed, almost without exception, that party identifiers have sorted on issues of the day, with Republicans moving to the right and Democrats to the left (but see Kinder and Kalmoe 2017, ch. 3). Our claim goes further. An accelerating share of Republicans are moving to the right, and an accelerating share of Democrats are moving to the left, programmatically and systematically.

How is this possible? Since the iconic Michigan election studies, it has been taken for granted that ideology is out of the reach of ordinary citizens (Campbell et al. 1960; Converse 1964). To be sure, scholars have pushed back against overdrawn claims. Numerous studies demonstrate that the political belief systems of the mass public have a substantial measure of coherence (Achen 1975; Ansolabehere, Rodden, and Snyder 2008; Carmines, Ensley, and Wagner 2012; Claggett and Shafer 2010; Erikson, MacKuen, and Stimson 2002; Feldman and Johnston 2014; Goren 2005; Shafer and Claggett 1995; but see Broockman 2016), and have become markedly more constrained and consistent in recent decades (Bafumi and Shapiro 2009; Kozlowski and Murphy 2021; Webster and Abramowitz 2017).

The question to ask is not categorical – can regular Democrats and Republicans take on board their party's policy commitments? – but contingent – under what conditions can partisans come to share the belief systems of their parties? Engagement with politics has been the most common answer – engagement expansively conceived to cover, variously, political interest, participation in campaigns, education, general political knowledge, and political sophistication (Abramowitz 2013; Barber and Pope 2018; Hare 2022; Lupton et al. 2015; Sniderman, Brody, and Tetlock 1991; Zaller 1992; Zingher 2022).

Political engagement is part of an answer to how politics gets polarized, but not the largest part. We find no evidence of a spike in political engagement sufficient to account for the spike in partisan polarization. Nor is there evidence of an upsurge of ordinary citizens who have mastered liberalism-conservatism as philosophies of politics. More sprinkle their likes and dislikes about parties with references to the "left" and "right," "liberal" and "conservative" nowadays, but the numbers who do so are hardly overwhelming (Allamong et al. n.d.; but see Wattenburg 2019, Fowler et al. n.d.). In any case, definitionally, ideology is a "cognitive structure capped by concepts of a high order of abstraction" that "permits the person to make sense of a broad range of political events" (Campbell et al. 1960, 193). No one, very much including us, supposes that a politically significant number of ordinary citizens have internalized a "cognitive structure" anything like this. How, then, can regular Republicans and Democrats become ideologically polarized?

Realism is our starting point. People do not start with an ideological lexicon in their head that they then deploy to organize and classify the swirl of their impressions of politics and public affairs into ideological categories. How things are organized and ordered in the world *is* their starting point. Political parties, via their candidates and programmatic advertising, provide holistic models of programmatically coherent belief systems. But *how*, exactly, can ordinary citizens use parties as holistic models of what goes with what and why?

1.4 Parties as Holistic Models: Framework Matching

Previous research provides guidance. First, consistent with mainstream views (e.g., Levendusky 2009, 2010), we treat polarization as top-down, with the parties-in-the-electorate in the main responding to the parties-in-government. "In the main" is key. It is a mistake to presume that polarization is either top-down or bottom-up. Here as elsewhere, the question to ask is, under what *conditions* is it one or the other? Most obviously, on a given issue or in a particular primary, voters may deliver a trumpeting verdict, compelling elites to react.[1] Then, too, as our results in Section 2.8 show, the parties-in-the-electorate can reinforce the polarization of the parties-in-government through the primary process. And most critically, to suppose that polarization is simply top-down is to miss the dynamics of partisan politics. Party supporters are not soldiers snapping to attention in response to their party leaders' commands, as the one-sided politics of race will drive home. But conceptual parsimony is a virtue. So we shall extract as much explanatory mileage as possible by treating partisan polarization as top-down.

The second lead from previous research is spot-on. An array of studies shows that knowing the parties' policy positions predicts whether someone will side

---

[1] For a compelling warning against a one-way conception of polarization, we are indebted to Eric Schickler, who called our attention to the example of then-House Majority Leader Eric Cantor's (R-VA) 2014 primary loss to David Brat, an obscure Tea Party candidate who criticized Cantor's willingness to compromise on immigration policy.

with their party on major issues (Levendusky 2009), take ideologically consistent positions across issues (Elder and O'Brian 2022), and develop more stable policy preferences (Freeder, Lenz, and Turney 2018).[2] Additional research shows that the consonance of political orientations matters too. For example, Goren, Federico, and Kittilson (2009) have shown that partisan cue-taking becomes more acute when partisans identify with their parties' ideological orientations – Republicans with conservatism, and Democrats with liberalism.

These results demonstrating, above all, the pivotal role of knowledge of the parties' positions, suggest a simple principle. Even politically active citizens are not all that active in politics: if they learn about politics, they learn by observing it, not by participating in it. The question then is, under what conditions can partisans take on board what the parties stand for by observing the play of politics?

One way to conceptualize the process of learning a political party's positions on issues is flat conditioning. So conceived, pairing the initially neutral stimulus, the party's position on an issue, with a positively valenced party generates a positively conditioned response. This is the nub of "issue sorting." Party supporters do not take a position on government health insurance because they have taken an ideologically compatible position on government activism in the economy, still less because they see both as sharing a common ideological provenance. On an issue sorting account, the policies are not connected together substantively. Instead, the learning is discrete issue by discrete issue, pairing the party's policy position with the party people identify with. No doubt, some learn their party's positions this way. But there are constraints on how much can be learned this way. The efficiency of learning by pairing is inversely related to the number of pairs to learn and to remember: the greater the number of pairs, the more costly encoding and retrieval.

Learning what goes with what in politics with any degree of comprehensiveness calls for a choice environment that is predictable and knowable. It is the business of political parties to organize and stabilize the choice environment. Ours is a simple idea: Learning by observing benefits from matching, similarity of a model and the observer of a model (cf. Bandura 1986, 48; 2023).[3] Partisans' overall orientation matching the overall outlook of their party, conservative if Republican, liberal if Democratic – puts them in a position to know what goes with what and why. A mismatch of frameworks – identifying as a Republican

---

[2] Freeder, Lenz, and Turney's (2018) results, showing that stable attitudes are conditional on knowledge of party positions, are a breakthrough response to the classic problem of non-attitudes.

[3] See Bandura (2023) for the most detailed and up-to-date overview. We are indebted to Christopher Hare for calling to our attention recent formal, and therefore general, models of similarity judgments in the learning process. See, for example, Gärdenfors (2000, 2020).

and a liberal, or a Republican without an ideological orientation – means you are looking in the wrong direction. Ditto identifying as a Democrat and a conservative, or a Democrat without an ideological orientation. Similarity of spatial orientation, Republicans orienting in the direction of their party, Democrats orienting themselves in the direction of their party, is thus the first condition for learning what the parties stand for programmatically.

Learning what goes with what and why goes beyond imitation or mimicry (Bandura 2023, 29–31). A measure of understanding, of getting the point, is also needed. Party supporters who know that they are oriented politically the same way their party is oriented, on our account, match their party's framework. Matching is the mechanism regulating partisan polarization.

Strong predictions follow, illustrated in Figure 2. First, party identifiers can be classified into two sets – matched partisans, party identifiers who are both emotionally attached to their party and share its political orientation; and *American Voter*-type partisans, party identifiers who are emotionally attached to their party but who support its policy commitments weakly, inconsistently, or not at all. Second, conditional on matching being the mechanism regulating partisan polarization, as the polarization of the parties-in-government makes the choice environment more readily knowable and predictable by sharpening the contrast between the two parties, the ratio of matched party identifiers (*core supporters* we shall call them) to *American Voter*-type party identifiers will increase. Third, and critically, partisan polarization will be circumscribed – indeed, to all intents and purposes confined to – Republicans and Democrats whose political orientation matches their party's. In contrast, their fellow Republicans and Democrats should move neither left nor right even as the centrifugal forces of polarization ratchet up.

1.5 An Overview

1.5.1 Over-Time Domain Dynamics

Electoral competition between the parties recurrently centers on three policy agendas: social welfare, racial, and cultural issues. As the positions of the parties-in-government have polarized, the positions of their supporters have converged across domains: if conservative on one, increasingly likely to be conservative on the others; if liberal on one, increasingly likely to be liberal on the others (Hare 2022). But this does not mean that polarization on each domain followed a common trajectory. Accordingly, our analysis tracks the distinctive over-time dynamics of the three agendas.

Issues of social welfare – how far the government should provide social assistance, and how far it is up to the individual to take care of the problems in

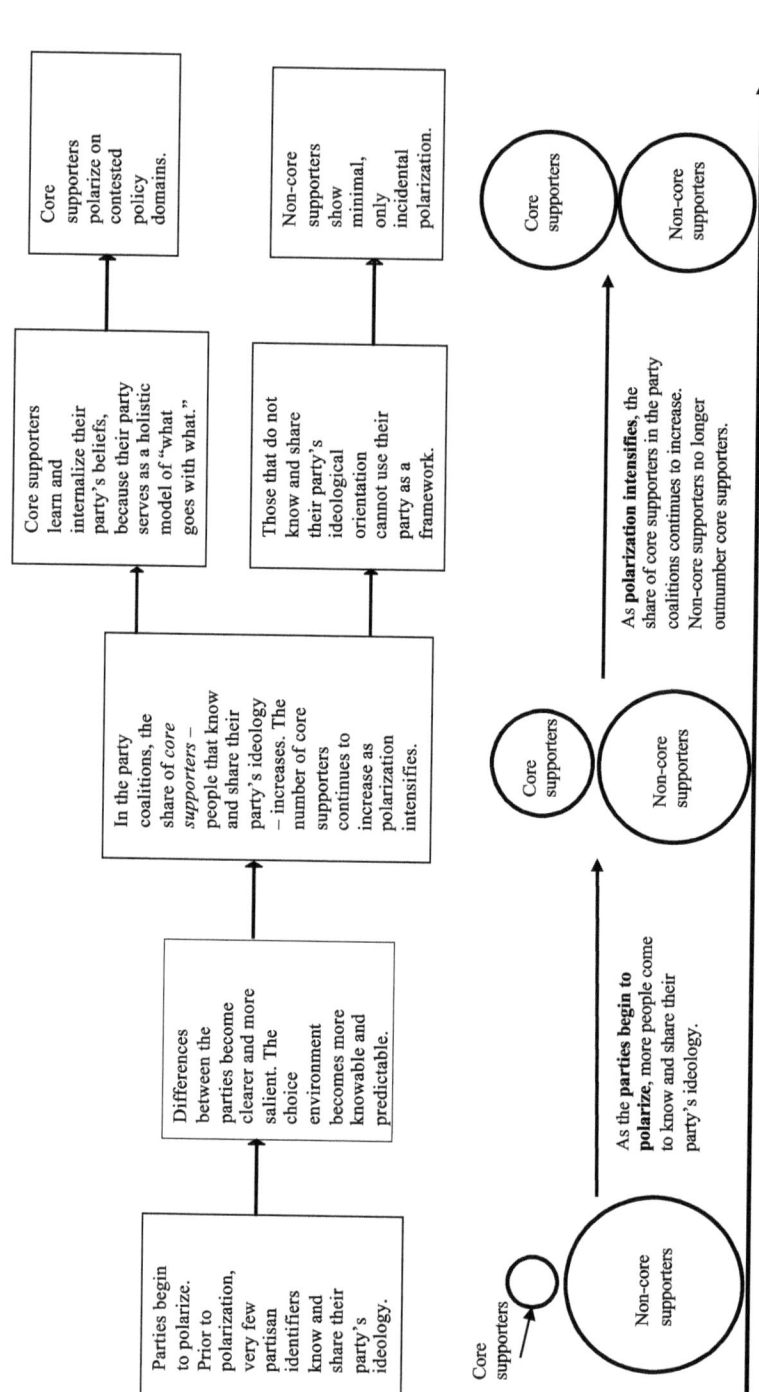

Figure 2 The logic of framework matching.

their life – have been the primary cleavage in the postwar United States (Claggett and Shafer 2010). It is, accordingly, not the least irony that social welfare politics rests on a quasi-consensus about government spending for long-established social services. As we show in Section 2.2.1, the largest number in both parties in the electorate oppose cuts to Social Security, childcare, and dealing with crime. In the face of this near-consensus, it cannot be a surprise that the Republican Party concentrates on contesting spending on unpopular social programs, welfare being the poster child (see Gilens 1999).

Exception noted, the parties-in-government square off against one another on a host of social welfare issues – among them, government health insurance, government intervention in the economy, and government services and spending broadly conceived. The key to the dynamics of polarization on social welfare politics is that the parties-in-government have battled one another over the scope of government since the New Deal. Their opposing positions on social welfare politics define their political identities.

The over-time dynamics of polarization on the social welfare agenda follow. As Section 2.2.2 demonstrates, core Republicans became steadily more conservative, and core Democrats steadily more liberal, with the gap between them progressively widening as elite polarization continued. Partisan polarization on the social welfare agenda was thus symmetrical, with supporters of both parties diverging from one another at the same rate and time, near as makes no difference.

The dynamics of racial politics are starkly different. Elite influence on Republicans' racial attitudes has been obvious, noted by an array of studies on the politics of race (e.g., Carmines and Stimson 1989; Layman and Carsey 2002; Sniderman and Carmines 1997; Tesler 2016; Valentino and Sears 2005). As the Republican party-in-government moved further right, so, too, did the Republican party-in-the-electorate. What has not been quite as obvious – indeed, what has to our knowledge been quite overlooked – is that the same is not true for (white) Democrats. In the mid-1960s, Democrats-in-government swung to the left on racial issues (Carmines and Stimson 1989). Then as the challenges of overcoming racial inequality became unmistakable, the Democratic Party committed itself to a more affirmative form of racial liberalism – backing affirmative action, racial set-asides in federal contracts, and majority-minority electoral districts. But the Democratic party-in-government, our results will show, could not bring even their core white supporters along with them. They stayed on the fence, for all practical purposes neutral on issues of race, and indeed on some like affirmative action conservative, through most of the period our data cover. The polarization of white Americans on issues of race was thus asymmetrical: core Republicans mobilized earlier and more comprehensively on issues of race. In sharp contrast, core Democrats have rallied to racial liberalism only in the last few years.

Rip tides are the mark of cultural politics. The antiwar counterculture of the 1960s and early 1970s could not find a footing in the larger society. Its brief surge sparked a backlash from the Religious Right. Religious conservatives mobilized in opposition to the Equal Rights Amendment – initially a bipartisan effort to recognize gender equality in the U.S. Constitution, by the early 1980s one of the touchstones of culture-war politics (Mansbridge 1986). The U.S. Supreme Court's decision in *Roe v. Wade* (1973) prompted a burgeoning of interest groups formed to reverse the Court's decision and promote alternatives to abortion (Lewis 2017; Luker 1985). Cultural issues transcended theological differences between conservative Protestants and Catholics, who united around support for traditional values (Layman 2001). Even against the decline of religious identification and attendance in American life, the Religious Right has become a wellspring of cultural conservatism.

Given the rip tides, asymmetries mark cultural politics. On abortion, core Democrats aligned with their party earlier than core Republicans; in the early 1980s, core Republicans were liberal on abortion, albeit less so than their Democratic counterparts. Core Republicans pivoted in the ensuing forty years, taking up a more conservative position on abortion. On gun control, core Republicans and Democrats were polarized in 2000, but core Democrats' support for gun control fluctuated significantly between 2004 and 2016. Differences in cultural values are even more telling. In 1986, the first year for which ANES data are available, core Republicans overwhelmingly favored more emphasis on traditional family values and rejected the idea that moral standards should evolve in response to social changes. Yet only in the mid-1990s did core Democrats leave the sidelines to take positions squarely at odds with moral traditionalism.

1.5.2 Polarization as Cohesion versus Divergence

Partisan polarization is standardly defined in terms of divergence, with Republicans becoming more conservative, and Democrats more liberal. An alternative conception is cohesion, more Republicans becoming conservative, more Democrats becoming liberal. The difference between the two conceptions of polarization is key to appreciating the party of the right's systematic advantage over the party of the left.

Figure 3 illustrates, for Republicans who know and share the ideological orientation of their party, the spatial logic of polarization. R_{t1} represents the position of the median Republican legislator before polarization, R_{t2} after

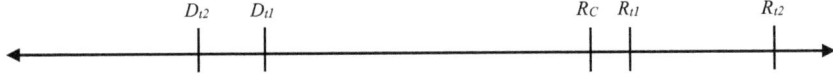

Figure 3 The spatial logic of polarization.

polarization; D_{t1} the position of the median Democratic legislator before polarization, D_{t2} after polarization; and R_c the median position of core Republicans both before and after polarization. Straightforwardly, the median Republican legislator is the spatial favorite of core Republicans before polarization: $(R_{t1} - R_c) < (D_{t1} - R_c)$. Equally straightforwardly, though, the median Republican legislator is the spatial favorite *even if the median Democratic legislator does not polarize*: $(R_{t2} - R_c) < (D_{t1} - R_c)$.

The logic of spatial voting, coupled with a reinterpretation of prior research, suggests that cohesion, not divergence, may be the key to which party has the upper hand and why in a polarized politics.

Previous studies have treated the increase in consistency between party identification and ideological identification as one more instance of issue sorting – instructive but not, in and of itself, more consequential than partisan sorting on a particular issue. In contrast, on our account, the key reason that party supporters support their party's programmatic agenda is that they know and share their party's ideological orientation. It is well known that Republicans are markedly more likely to identify as conservatives than Democrats are to identify as liberals (e.g., Ellis and Stimson 2012; Levendusky 2009). If party supporters' political outlook matching their party's is the key to their backing their party's policies, as we hypothesize, Republicans will be systematically more cohesive than Democrats on issues the parties contest. In turn, given the strict logic of spatial voting, the Republican Party will have a greater latitude than the Democratic Party to push its policies to the limit.[4]

1.6 Implications

Our recurring theme is that, for an accelerating number of Republicans and Democrats, polarization has made politics substantive. If true, what else is true? A claim about the immediacy of the connection between emotions and beliefs comes first. From one perspective, polarization is all about emotions, above all, the spike in negative feelings toward the opposing party (Diermeier and Li 2019; Iyengar and Krupenkin 2018; Iyengar, Sood, and Lelkes 2012; Mason

---

[4] It is worth underlining that no empirical analysis supports the logical possibility that, if one party polarizes, the other will counter-polarize (e.g., the Democratic Party becoming less liberal, the Republican Party less conservative) to capture the median vote.

2014, 2018). From another perspective, it is about beliefs, above all, consistent beliefs across issues sharing a common rationale (Ansolabehere, Rodden, and Snyder 2008; Carmines, Ensley, and Wagner 2012; Claggett and Shafer 2010; Shafer and Claggett 1995). The two perspectives are commonly treated as rivals. Either emotion is integral and belief peripheral (Iyengar, Sood, and Lelkes 2012; Iyengar and Westwood 2015; see also Mason 2018), or belief is integral and emotion peripheral (Costa 2021; Orr and Huber 2020).

Our choice is to follow the lead of a third body of studies that stresses the connection between political emotions and political beliefs (e.g., Dias and Lelkes 2022; Rogowski and Sutherland 2016; Webster and Abramowitz 2017). Following their lead and taking a step further is the plan. In politics, emotion and belief are not merely connected. When genuine, they are entangled, inextricably. The imagery of one as a cause, the other an effect, is a conceptual snare. What could it mean to truly believe that affirmative action is morally required to overcome centuries of racial injustice, yet be indifferent when the Court struck it down? What could it mean to truly believe that abortion is the murder of an unborn child, yet be indifferent when the Supreme Court declared it legally permissible? In politics, to believe is to believe *in*.

Our analysis of the over-time dynamics of partisan polarization centers on the upsurge of partisans who know and share the ideological orientation of their party. They know what it stands for. They stand with it. They know what is at stake should it lose. And because they not merely believe, but believe *in* what their party stands for, their convictions and their feelings are opposite sides of the same coin.

But what type of beliefs and feelings are they? Since Converse's masterwork, "The Nature of Belief Systems in Mass Publics" (1964), public opinion studies have presumed that political ideologies like liberalism and conservatism are outside the reach of ordinary citizens. Citizens, the textbook argument runs, lack the political engagement and sophistication that would enable them to reason through the superordinate principles that define a political ideology. In contrast, our claim is that regular Republicans and Democrats *can* take on board their party's programmatic commitments if they know and share its ideological orientation. On issues the parties contest, core Republicans will consistently and predictably take conservative positions, and Democrats will consistently and predictably take liberal positions.

To claim that some large number of Republicans are conservatives and Democrats liberals is not to claim that they are ideologues, reasoning from first principles. To be a conservative or liberal is to have a determinate predisposition to consistently and predictably express conservative or liberal ideas, support conservative or liberal policies, and vote for conservative or liberal candidates and parties. Republicans who know and share the political orientation of their party know they are conservatives, know that their party is the conservative party – and consistently and systematically support conservative policies. They are conservatives in fact and not just in name. Democrats who know and share the political orientation of their party know that their party is the liberal party, that they are liberals – and, with the exception of race until very recently, consistently and systematically support liberal policies. They are liberals in fact and not just in name. Accordingly, without wishing to be provocative, just so far as the Republican and Democratic parties-in-government have become ideologically polarized, we regard Democrats and Republicans who affirm their party's tenets faithfully and consistently stand behind its programmatic commitments as ideological partisans.

A final – and radical – implication of our approach needs calling out. Two interpretations of party identification currently command the most support. One, introduced by *The American Voter* (Campbell et al. 1960), is that party identification, at its core, represents an emotional attachment with minimal policy content. The other is that party identification has become "more ideological and more issue based along liberal-conservative lines than it has been in more than 30 years" (Bafumi and Shapiro 2009, 1; see also Abramowitz 2010; Campbell 2016; Schier and Eberly 2016). Research has proceeded as though one or the other is right. Our position is that both interpretations are right. That may have the appearance of being merely conciliatory, an expression of academic good manners. In fact, the implication is radical. Party identification means one thing to some party identifiers and something quite different to others.

For many, even in a polarized politics, to identify with a party is to be emotionally attached to it and not much more. But in a polarized politics, for many Democrats and Republicans, to identify with their party goes beyond being emotionally attached to it. To be a Republican is to be a conservative, and not just in name; to be a Democrat is to be a liberal, and not just in name. This claim of heterogeneity – that to identify with a political party means two quite different things – has a far-reaching implication. It calls for distinguishing between two types of party identifiers; indeed, analyzing them *separately*, depending on whether their connection to their party is emotional and not much more, or programmatic as well as emotional. This is a radical departure from previous research, which is all the more reason to underline how far our approach is indebted to and follows from previous research, beginning with Levendusky's pioneering analyses of issue sorting (2009, 2010).

2 Dynamics of Partisan Polarization

Policy divergence is a hallmark of partisan polarization, with Republicans consistently to the right and Democrats to the left. However, because the policy preferences of each party's supporters have converged on a common dimension, it does not follow that they have tracked a common trajectory. Our focus, accordingly, is on the distinctive dynamics of mass partisan polarization on social welfare, cultural, and racial issues.

To preview our results, social welfare politics is New Deal politics only more so. Core Republicans and Democrats were polarized on social welfare issues at least as early as 1972, the first year that the ANES asked about ideological self-identification – polarizing over the next fifty years at about the same time and pace, especially on the question of government health insurance. Racial politics tells a different story. From the early 1970s to the most recent election cycles, polarization on race was asymmetrical. Racial conservatism, limited government intervention to assist Blacks, was a congenial fit for white Republicans who favored limited government on social welfare issues. In contrast, racial liberalism, active government intervention to help Blacks, has proven a challenge for white Democrats – very much including white liberal Democrats. Finally, while polarization in cultural politics is marked by asymmetries too, these do not consistently favor one party over the other. For example, Republicans embraced moral traditionalism long before Democrats moved toward greater acceptance of changing cultural norms, while Democrats had consolidated around support for abortion rights before most Republicans took an anti-abortion position.

2.1 From Conceptualization to Measurement

Under what conditions will supporters of a party take on board, not their party's position on this or that issue, but the overall program of policies it advances within a policy domain? Knowing your party's policies and programmatic approach must be part of the answer, but more is required. It is necessary to understand, to internalize, to draw correct inferences. How is this possible for an ordinary citizen who pays attention to politics irregularly and often only superficially?

Section 1.3 set out a theory of *framework matching, Republicans and Democrats orienting themselves to match their party*. The challenge now is to operationalize it. Tracking the temporal dynamics of the polarization of the parties-in-the electorate is the objective. The longer and more continuous the period of coverage, the better. The American National Election Studies, the gold standard of surveys in political science, is unmistakably the best choice; most of our analysis relies on the cumulative data file (ANES 2022). Operationalization of framework matching follows straightforwardly. Similarity of spatial orientation is assessed by the consistency of party[5] and ideological identification,[6] conceptualized and measured the same way since 1972. To assess consistency, we look for whether Republicans identify as conservatives and Democrats as liberals. Party placement questions on specific issues vary from election to election,[7] but in each midterm and election-year study since 1972, the ANES has asked respondents to place the parties on the liberal-conservative spectrum. Accordingly, as an indicator of understanding, we opt for knowledge of the parties' relative positions on the liberal-conservative spectrum[8] – whether respondents placed the Republican Party to the right of the Democratic Party on the traditional, seven-point scale.

---

[5] We code respondents as Republicans and Democrats using the traditional, seven-point scale used on the ANES. Consistent with standard practice, respondents were coded as partisans if they identified as strong partisans, weak partisans, or partisan "leaners" (that is, people that initially called themselves independents but reported that they felt closer to one of the two parties). While partisan "leaners" feel more ambivalent about their party than strong and weak partisans (Klar and Krupnikov 2016), their voting behavior and issue positions are much more consistent with partisan identifiers than with pure independents (Abramowitz 2015, 25–26; Keith et al. 1992). That said, no differences of consequence were observed in parallel analyses classifying leaners as independents.

[6] We code respondents as "conservatives" if they identified as slightly conservative, conservative, or extremely conservative on the standard, seven-point scale; and "liberals" if they identified as slightly liberal, liberal, or extremely liberal. Our coding is based only on respondents' answers to the initial self-identification question; while some ANES modules asked respondents which ideological orientation they would choose if they had to pick, "forced choice" questions of this nature are unlikely to give an accurate sense of whether respondents share their party's ideological orientation.

[7] Party placement on government guaranteed jobs was asked consistently between 1972 and 2020 – but unlike ideological self-identification, the question is hardly a stand-in for the parties' ideological orientations in general. Meanwhile, respondents were asked to place the parties on government health insurance in only seven of the last twenty-one elections, omitting 2016 and 2020. Party placement on government aid to Blacks has not been asked since 2004. Party placement on government services and spending appeared more frequently prior to 2000, but was not asked in 2004, 2008, 2016, or 2020. In recent cycles, *candidate* placement questions have been more common. However, both theoretically and empirically, these are fundamentally different from party placement questions. We have theorized that for partisans that know and share their party's ideological orientation, parties serve as models of coherent belief systems. But candidates come and go too quickly to be models for observational learning. Moreover, because they match their party's ideology and understand that a victory for their party is a victory for the *party's* ideology, core supporters might discount the significance of candidate ideology (Sniderman and Stiglitz 2012).

[8] From 1972 to 1996, the ANES did not ask respondents to place the parties on the liberal-conservative spectrum unless they were willing to identify themselves with an ideological orientation (whether liberal, conservative, or moderate). For this time period, we code as *unmatched partisans* people that did not claim an ideological orientation and were thus not shown the party placement questions; treating these respondents as missing data would otherwise eliminate hundreds of cases from the relevant cross-sections. Because partially matched and unmatched partisans often differ negligibly on the attitudes we investigate, this decision has minimal effect on our analyses – and no effect on our analysis of the attitudes of matched partisans.

Matching is a matter of degree, which our measure captures to only a limited degree.[9] *Fully matched partisans* are Democrats and Republicans who know and share their parties' ideological orientation[10]; *partially matched partisans* are Democrats and Republicans who either identify with the ideological orientation of their party but do not know it, or know it but do not identify with it; and *unmatched partisans* are Democrats and Republicans who neither know nor identify with their party's ideological orientation. Modest claims in measurement should be the order of the day for survey research all in all, modesty-cubed for secondary analysis of public opinion surveys. It is our hope that, if our approach is found useful, subsequent research will develop superior measures of framework matching.

2.1.1 Framework Matching as a Mechanism of Polarization

Our claim is that partisans matching the ideological framework of their party is the mechanism regulating the use of the parties as holistic models of what goes with what programmatically. Two predictions in particular follow. First, as the parties-in-government polarize on policy, the proportion of partisan identifiers who know and share their party's orientation will increase too. Second, only *matched* partisan identifiers will polarize in response to elite polarization, because they alone have the incentive and knowledge to use their party as a holistic model of what goes with what.

Testing the first prediction, Figure 4[11] tracks the proportions of party identifiers who know and share their party's ideological orientation, from 1972 through 2020.[12]

---

[9] One word fewer in a frequently repeated phrase is an economy not to be sneezed at. So we shall commonly shorten "framework matching" to "matching."

[10] Again valuing brevity, we shall refer to them simply as *matched partisans*, and for variety, sometimes as *core supporters*.

[11] All statistical analyses were conducted in R (R Development Core Team 2008), using the jtools package (Long 2022). Graphs were generated using ggplot2 (Wickham 2016).

[12] Especially in recent years, the overwhelming majority of matched partisans have placed the Republican Party to the right-of-center and the Democratic Party to the left-of-center on the seven-point scales. For example, in 2020, only 5 percent of matched Republicans did not identify the Republican Party as "slightly conservative," "conservative," or "extremely conservative"; of these, most said the Republican Party was "moderate" and that the Democratic Party was one of the liberal options. Similarly, only 14.1 percent of matched Democrats did not identify the Democratic Party as "slightly liberal," "liberal," or "extremely liberal"; of these, most said the Democratic Party was "moderate" and that the Republican Party was one of the conservative options. Most matched partisans understand the parties' ideological reputations in both absolute *and* relative terms. Beyond this, skeptical readers might wonder whether some people misidentify their party's ideological orientation and identify with *this* orientation, even though they place the Republican Party to the right of the Democratic Party on the seven-point scales. For example, suppose that a Democratic identifier says that the Democratic Party is "moderate" and the Republican

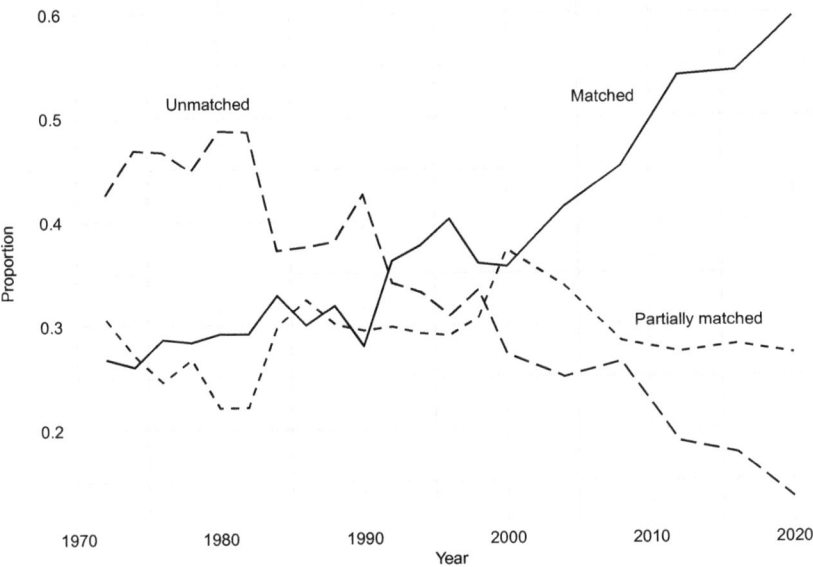

Figure 4 Matching, 1972–2020. The lines refer to the proportion of partisan identifiers composed of each group. Respondents are classified as *matched partisans* if they shared their party's ideological orientation and correctly placed the parties on the liberal-conservative spectrum. Data: ANES cumulative file, partisan identifiers only.

From 1972 to 1990, about 30 percent of partisans matched the ideological framework of their party. Beginning during the Clinton administration, this figure began to climb. After the 2000 election, it rocketed up. By 2020, a majority of partisans were in ideological sync with their party (see also Fiorina 2017, 79–85).

Figure 4 is evidence consistent with framework matching as a mechanism for the polarization of the parties-in-the-electorate. However, tests of a hypothesis must be double-edged, ruling out plausible alternative hypotheses as well as reporting results consistent with the favored hypothesis. The most plausible alternative mechanism is political interest and awareness. Indeed, Abramowitz (2010, 2013) argues that polarization has been

---

Party "extremely conservative," and calls themselves a "moderate" at the same time. This person would be coded as *partially matched* because they understand the spatial logic of the party system, but do not identify with their party's "liberal" orientation. This profile describes only a small minority, happily, (e.g., less than 5 percent in 2020) of partisan identifiers. We are indebted to L.J. Zigerell for suggesting this robustness check on our results.

confined to an "engaged public," largely defined in terms of political interest and participation. For their part, Barber and Pope (2018) find that political knowledge outperforms other measures of political sophistication in promoting issue constraint (see also Lupton, Myers, and Thornton 2015). Fortunately, the ANES provides a variety of indicators of political sophistication – among them, political knowledge (both measured objectively and rated by interviewers), interest in public affairs, educational attainment, interest in elections, and participation in campaign-related activities (i.e., low-level activism).[13]

Figure 4 shows that partisan matching shot up after 2000. Figure 5 stands in stark contrast. Democrats and Republicans have *not* become markedly more likely to report that they follow public affairs "most of the time." Nor have they become markedly more likely to participate in various campaign-related activities or become better informed about politics (measured in terms of general political knowledge questions or subjective interviewer ratings in face-to-face interviews). They have become more likely to say that they are "very much interested" in elections – whatever it might mean to say this without becoming better informed about politics, or following politics more closely, or becoming more involved in campaigns and elections. Similarly, core supporters (especially core Democrats) have become more likely to attend college – but their educational attainment has hardly made them more likely to engage in campaign-related activities. Simply put, matching has rocketed up as politics has polarized; substantive political engagement has not.[14]

Now, for the second prediction: If matching is the mechanism for partisan polarization as we hypothesize, then party supporters taking on board their party's policy programs will be conditional on their sharing their party's ideological orientation.

---

[13] Most measures of political sophistication recur throughout the fifty-year period our data cover. The exception is knowledge of political facts and figures, for which the questions often vary in breadth and depth. The measure of general political knowledge in Figure 5 was based on four questions, recurring in 1992, 1996, 2004, 2008, 2012, 2016, and 2020. These asked respondents to identify the office held by the (then-current) vice president, Speaker of the House, and Chief Justice of the United States, and to identify which party held a majority in the House of Representatives before the most recent election.

[14] Hersh (2020) puts forward an alternative paradigm, "political hobbyism," by which people become superficially invested in politics but without the substantive engagement associated with meaningful participation. We doubt that framework matching can be reduced to political hobbyism, because matching is only modestly correlated with the more superficial measures of sophistication in Figure 5. For example, in 2020 the tetrachoric correlation between matching and interest in the elections was only 0.28; matching correlated with educational attainment and general political knowledge at only 0.38 and 0.42, respectively.

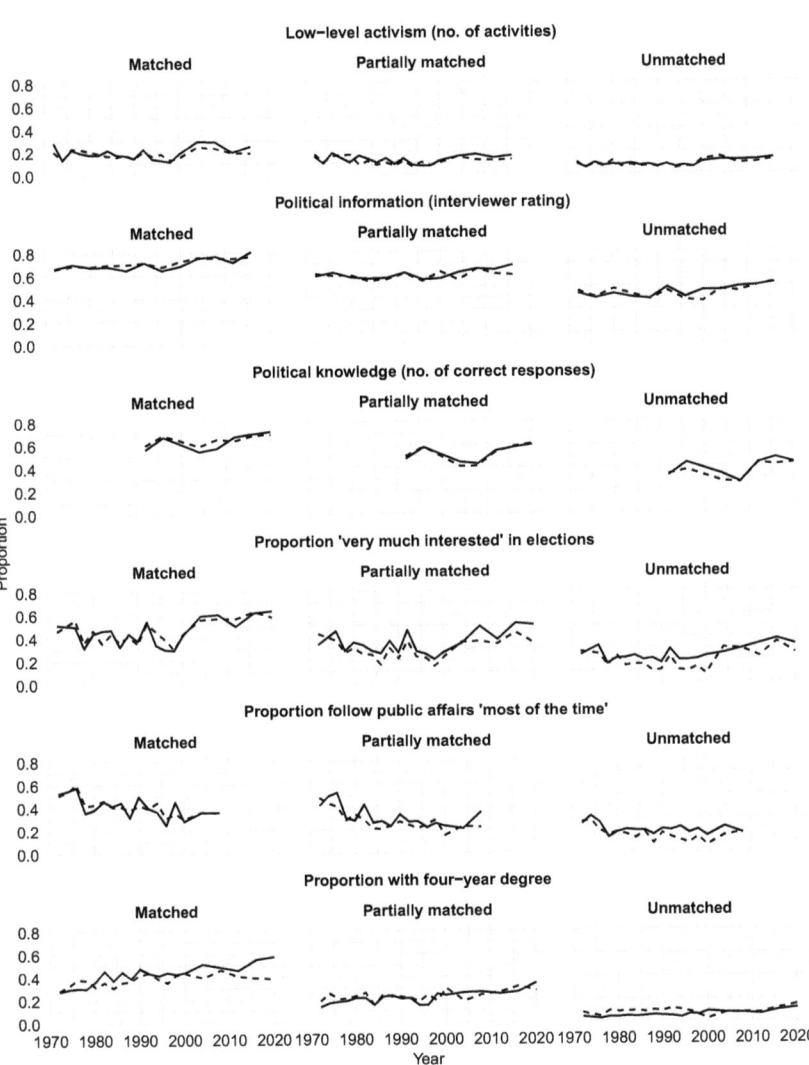

Figure 5 Alternate metrics of political sophistication, 1972–2020. All continuous variables were rescaled to range between 0 and 1. Data: ANES cumulative file, partisan identifiers only.

2.2 Social Welfare/Scope of Government Politics

Catching hold of the spirit of democratic politics requires an openness to irony. Among other examples: It is simultaneously true that social welfare politics operates at two levels – most obviously contested, less obviously quasi-consensual. What is less obvious deserves attention first.

2.2.1 Quasi-consensus on Social Services

History matters. Since the New Deal, contending views about the scope of government in assuring the social welfare of citizens have been the primary battleground. Responding to the Great Depression, FDR's New Deal innovated on many fronts, among them, enhanced social welfare and assistance programs (e.g., minimum wages and Social Security), government regulation of the economy, and public ownership of natural resources and energy facilities (e.g., the Tennessee Valley Authority) (Katznelson 2014). Truman's Fair Deal expanded federal assistance (e.g., increasing Social Security benefits), pioneering antidiscrimination legislation in the process.

From Eisenhower on, the Republican Party has accepted the legitimacy of a broad array of New Deal-inspired social services (Kabaservice 2012; Rae 1989). Indeed, the GOP has extended some – perhaps most dramatically through the construction of the Interstate Highway System.[15] To be sure, the parties have intermittently clashed over levels of spending for established social services – with the Democratic Party calling for more, and the Republican party for less. Yet the GOP has tacitly accepted the status quo and, indeed, occasionally capitalized on the electoral payoff for introducing new social benefits and services. Thus, for example, under George W. Bush's Medicare Modernization Act, Medicare services were expanded to include outpatient prescription drugs – a significant expansion of a flagship entitlement program. Broad bipartisan support for spending on long-established social services is a safe prediction.

Figure 6 charts opposition to decreased spending, from 1984 through 2020, on three exemplary categories of social services – Social Security, childcare, and dealing with crime.[16] Opposition to cuts is near-unanimous. It does not matter whether partisan supporters know and identify with their party's ideological orientation. For that matter, it is irrelevant whether they identify as Democrats or Republicans. Of course, core Republicans are less likely than core Democrats to oppose cuts in childcare spending. Yet that is because, with the exception of 2012 when opposition fell to 58 percent, "only" about 75 percent of core Republicans oppose cuts – compared to about 91 percent of everyone else. And yes, core Democrats in 2020 became less opposed to cutting spending for crime prevention, presumably in response to the murder of George Floyd and the resurgence of the Black Lives Matter movement. Yet recent events – notably, Minneapolis voters' rejection of a 2021 ballot initiative to

---

[15] For two authoritative histories of the New Deal and the moderate wing of the Republican Party under Dwight Eisenhower (respectively), see Katznelson (2014) and Rae (1989).
[16] The item on childcare appeared for the last time in 2016.

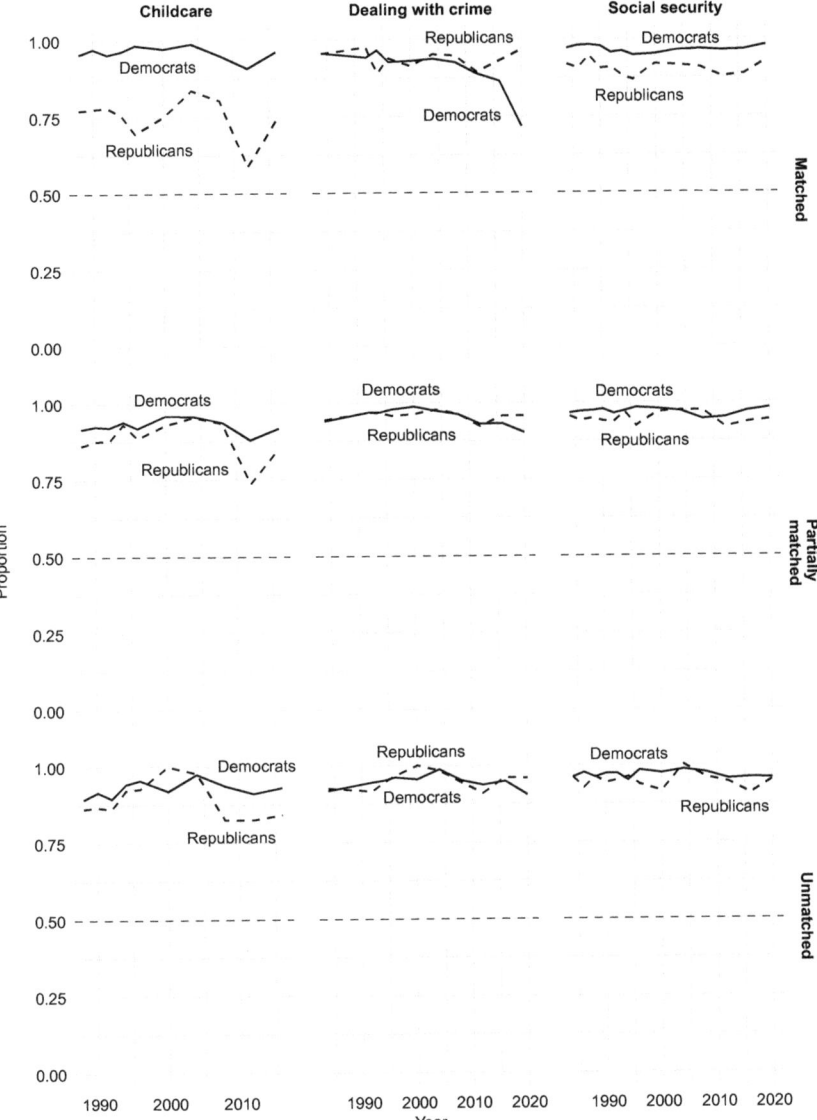

Figure 6 Proportion that oppose decreased spending on federal programs, 1984–2020, by partisanship and matching status. The dashed line indicates 50 percent; the plots illustrate the proportions of each group that said spending should be increased or kept the same. Data: ANES cumulative file, partisan identifiers only.

eliminate the city's police department (Olapido 2021) – suggest that Democrats' support for spending cuts has been short-lived. Polling tells a similar story; according to the Pew Research Center, white Democrats' support for police funding increased markedly between June 2020 and October 2021 (Parker and Hurst 2021) – suggesting that the quasi-consensus on crime prevention and policing has begun to reemerge. In any case, far and away the largest number of core Democrats remain opposed to cutting spending on dealing with crime. Support for spending on established social services is quasi-consensual.[17]

2.2.2 Polarization as Policy Divergence

The concept of polarization is systematically ambiguous. Viewed from one perspective, it flags policy divergence, with Republicans becoming more conservative and Democrats more liberal, one or both possibly extremely so. Viewed from another, it signals party cohesion, with more Republicans becoming conservative and more Democrats becoming liberal. We take them in turn.

Polarization of the parties-in-the-electorate, standardly envisioned, is symmetrical: Republicans becoming progressively more conservative, Democrats progressively more liberal, at the same time and the same rate nearly enough.[18] Policy divergence, the gap between the two on social welfare policy, thus serves as a measure of polarization; the wider the gap, the more intense the polarization.

Social welfare politics, though quasi-consensual at the level of long-established social services, is highly conflictual in the frontline trenches. The Democratic Party champions more government activism in the economy, higher tax rates for the well-off, and more public assistance for the disadvantaged. The Republican Party champions economic deregulation, lower taxes, and reduced government spending. So it has been and so it continues to be, and still more so in a polarized politics where both parties have notched up trophy achievements. Under Obama, the Democratic Party passed the Affordable Care Act, the largest expansion in access to health insurance since LBJ's Great Society reforms. During Donald Trump's first term, the Republican Party legislated major changes in tax liabilities, significantly reducing levies on corporations and the wealthy.[19]

---

[17] Which is not to say that spending for all social services is quasi-consensual, welfare being the counterexample that comes immediately to mind (see Gilens 1999).

[18] An assumption of symmetry is built-in to the use of correlation coefficients to estimate sorting.

[19] The standard designations for the two levels, operational and symbolic (see Ellis and Stimson 2012), are not apt in our view. The "symbolic" level carries the connotation that what is at issue is abstract and performative, rather than programmatic. Healthcare policies are "operational" by any standard; so too are government programs to combat unemployment; and so too are judgments about overall levels of spending for government services. A different issue is abstraction (e.g., attitudes towards Obamacare) and mandate bundling (e.g., attitudes towards specific provisions of Obamacare). For an inventive and compelling analysis of the limits of top-down influence on attitudes towards policy framed in abstract terms and specific provisions, see Hopkins (2023).

How have the parties-in-the-electorate responded? Figure 7 denotes the average positions of partisan identifiers on three emblematic social welfare issues: government-guaranteed jobs, government services and spending, and government health insurance. The dashed line tracks Republican identifiers, and the solid line tracks Democratic identifiers.[20]

Both parties have made their opposing positions clear from the New Deal onward. Unsurprisingly, then, the dynamics of the three issues are the same.[21] Core Republicans and Democrats diverged on social welfare issues as early as 1972, and they diverged further as party politics polarized. Consistent with the popular picture of polarization, symmetric polarization is the mark of ideological conflict on the social welfare agenda.

Matching, Figure 7 suggests, is the mechanism governing partisan polarization – providing a first hint that accounting for matching brings to light what the established picture of polarization misses. Polarization is concentrated among, indeed for all practical purposes restricted to, core supporters of the parties. In contrast, even as the positions of the parties-in-government have increasingly and assertively diverged on the social welfare agenda, differences on social welfare issues have remained minimal for Republicans and Democrats who do not fully match their party's ideological orientation.

2.2.3 Polarization as Party Cohesion

Figure 7 shows that on social welfare issues, partisan divergence has been concentrated among – indeed, nearly enough confined to – Republicans and Democrats whose overall outlook matches their party's. Yet given the spatial logic of polarization (see Figure 3), party cohesion offers a more telling way to determine who has the upper hand and why.

If matching is the mechanism regulating the polarization of the parties-in-the-electorate, the success of the parties-in-government in increasing the proportion of their supporters whose ideological orientation matches their party's is critical. Figure 8 accordingly tracks the upsurge of matching for Democrats and Republicans separately. The sheer size of the gap, at every point in time, stands out. Until 2004, less than 30 percent of Democrats were core supporters; not until 2020 did core supporters constitute the slim majority of Democratic

---

[20] We use the standard seven-point scales that have historically appeared on the American National Election Studies, rescaled between 0 and 1. Respondents who said that they "haven't thought much about this" were coded at the midpoint. Higher average values indicate more conservative responses. Complete question wording is found in the online appendix.

[21] Caution is in order in interpreting absolute levels of support for the liberal position on the government guaranteed jobs item, given its extreme wording. Respondents are asked whether "the government in Washington should see to it that every person has a job and a good standard of living" or whether "the government should just let each person get ahead on his/her own."

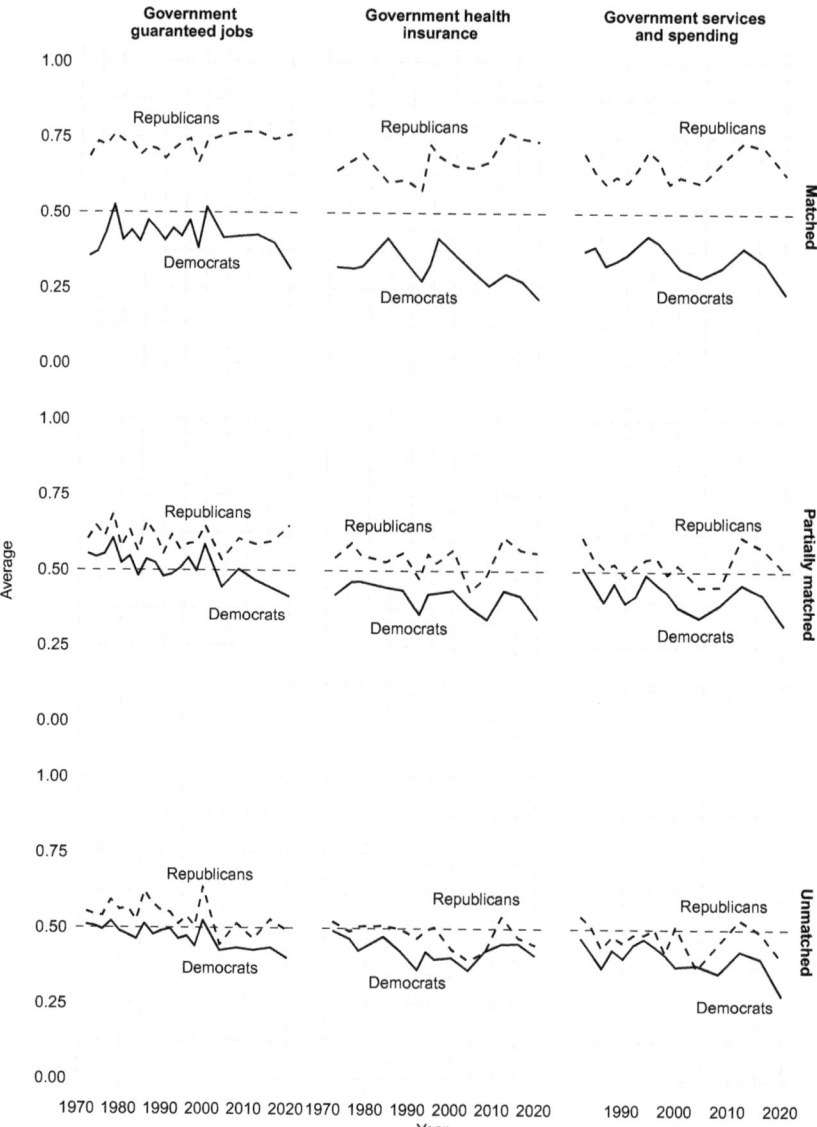

Figure 7 Average attitudes on the size and scope of government, 1972–2020, by partisanship and matching status. Higher scores indicate more conservative attitudes; all variables were rescaled between 0 and 1. The dashed lines indicate the midpoints on the seven-point scales. Data: ANES cumulative file, partisan identifiers only.

identifiers. Over the same period, the proportion of Republicans who were core supporters was often *twice* the proportion of Democrats who were core supporters.

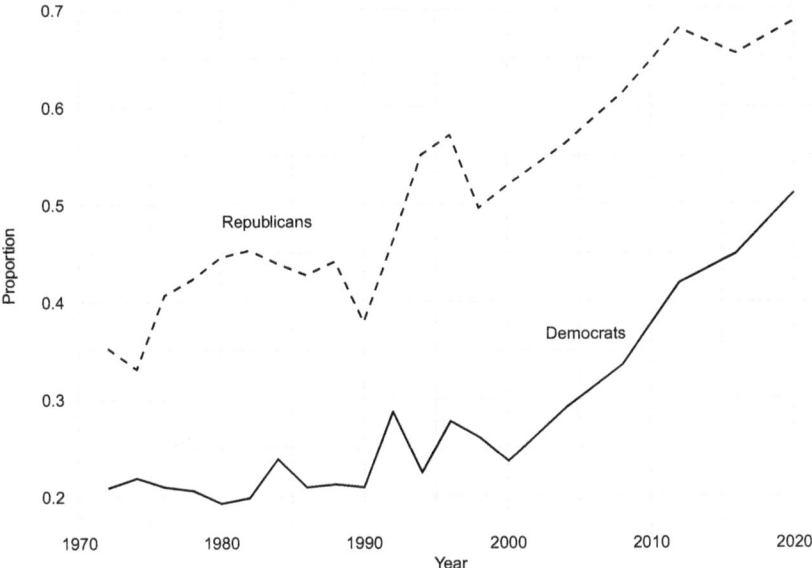

Figure 8 Matching rates by partisanship, 1972–2020. The lines refer to the proportion of Republican or Democratic identifiers that both shared their party's ideological orientation and correctly placed the parties on the liberal-conservative spectrum. Data: ANES cumulative file.

It follows that, at every point, Republicans will be more cohesive, more likeminded, on issues the parties contest. But as we worked through our thinking, we were pricked by a concern. The positions that a party takes, not just the fact that they have taken a position, matter.

On some issues, the positions that the parties have taken will have a comparable appeal to their supporters, near as makes no practical difference. But on others, the positions that one party takes may have a stronger appeal to their supporters than the positions of the opposing party have to theirs. It follows that, to gauge the cohesion of the two parties we must estimate a conditional probability – the likelihood that a Republican or Democratic identifier both knows and identifies with their party's ideological orientation and takes their party's side on a contested issue. Expressed formally:

$P(\text{Matched} \cap \text{Issue Sorted} \mid \text{Republican})$

$P(\text{Matched} \cap \text{Issue Sorted} \mid \text{Democrat})$

The greater the conditional probability, the more cohesive the party is on that issue.

Polarization – defined as policy divergence – is symmetrical on social welfare issues. Core Republicans become more conservative, core Democrats become more liberal, at the same time and the same rate nearly enough (Figure 7). However, while policy divergence on social welfare is symmetrical, polarization in terms of party cohesion is asymmetrical. Figure 9 shows how Republicans' advantage in core supporters cashes out in a substantive advantage on social welfare issues – specifically, a larger portion of supporters who both match their party's ideological orientation and take the generally conservative position on various issues.

For the three social welfare policies, Figure 9 charts the cohesiveness of Republican (dashed line) and Democratic (black line) core supporters from the earliest available data point to 2020. Polarization conceptualized as party cohesion sharply increased for both parties after 2000.[22] But what is politically telling is the disparity between the parties. Republicans were markedly more cohesive than Democrats on social welfare issues – in many elections, between two to three times as cohesive – *before* American politics began to polarize. Astonishingly, Democrats became markedly more cohesive on social welfare issues only in the last few election cycles – and on only one issue, government services and spending, have they matched the cohesiveness of their Republican counterparts. This polarization lag – the Republican Party mustering its core supporters early and comprehensively, the Democratic Party only in the last few years – reflects a politically telling asymmetry in the politics of social welfare.

2.3 The Politics of Race

Top-down politics, with party supporters following their party's leaders, is the accepted story of the politics of polarization. But politics is not simply top-down, with partisan supporters standing at attention to receive orders. The positions that a party takes, not merely the fact that it takes them, matter. This is nowhere clearer than in the differences on racial issues between white Democrats and Republicans.[23]

---

[22] Close readers will note that in many cases, the 2000 election cycle is an outlier in the attitudinal trends we document – marking a dip in party cohesion, for example, that resurged dramatically by 2004. We suspect two reasons for this dip, one historical, the other an artifact of the unique nature of the 2000 ANES. First, the 2000 presidential election might well be remembered as the last time the presidential candidates actively competed for the ideological center. Second, and perhaps more on-point, the 2000 ANES included various split-ballot experiments (some involving the policy scales we use to estimate attitudes on social welfare spending), radically reducing the number of cases for analysis.

[23] And not only of race. Hopkins (2023) provides a deep account of the limits of top-down politics in organizing public opinion on the Affordable Care Act.

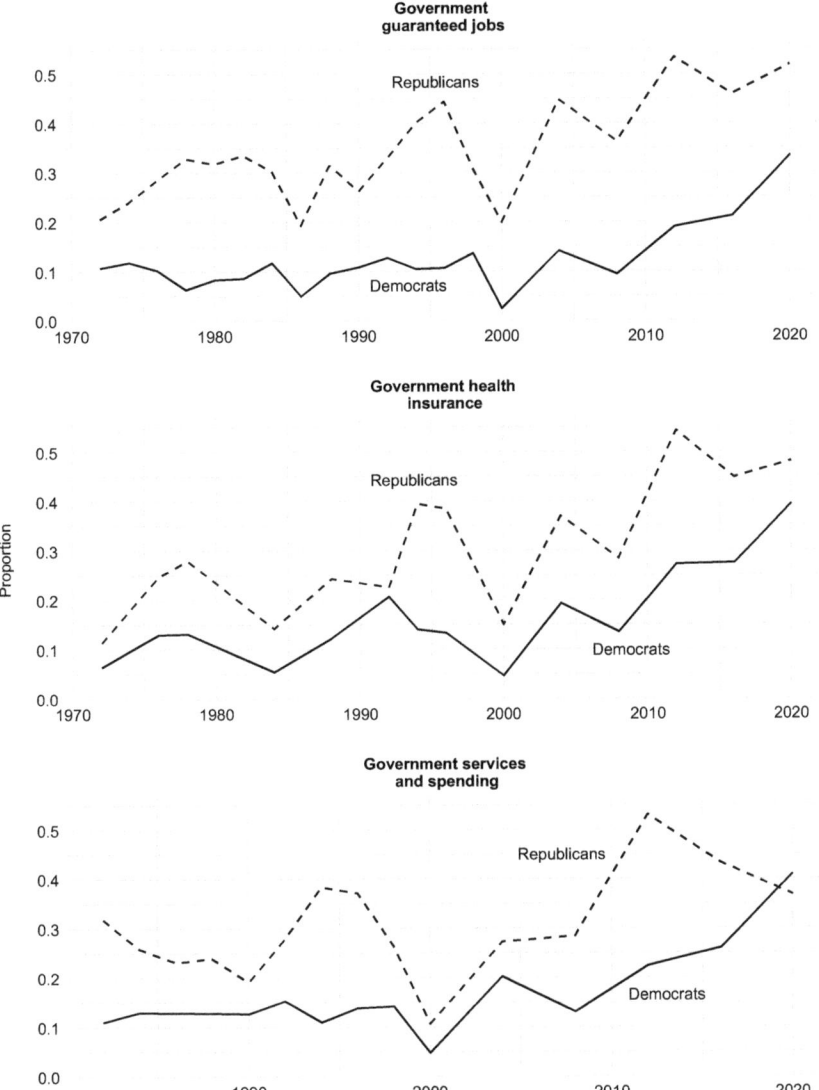

Figure 9 Party cohesion on social welfare issues: matched and issue-sorted partisans in the party coalitions, 1972–2020. The plots show the proportions of Republican and Democratic identifiers that both matched their party's ideological orientation and shared their party's position on each issue. Data: ANES cumulative file.

The Civil Rights Act of 1964, the Voting Rights Act of 1965, and the Fair Housing Act of 1968 were apex achievements of the Civil Rights Movement. A crescendo of race riots, exploding in Watts, Detroit, and Newark, ultimately erupting in over a hundred American cities, scarred the last half of the 1960s.

The rise of Black Power and Black Nationalism virtually gutted cross-racial coalitions. The Democratic Party had been the party of the working class. Then, in the vocabulary of the Left, the working class became the *white* working class, and for many in the white working class, the Democratic Party became the party of Blacks. From the 1970s on, Democratic politicians and activists continued to campaign against systemic racial inequalities, publicly backing *unpopular* policies in the name of racial justice – most controversially, busing and affirmative action. The result: A deep disconnect on racial politics between the Democratic Party in government and core white supporters who remained sympathetic to the party's social welfare policies.

2.3.1 Polarization as Policy Divergence

If any policy battleground fits the popular idea of polarization as the politics of passionate extremes, it is race. This is true for the parties-in-government but false for the parties-in-the-electorate. The left column of Figure 10 traces white Republicans' and Democrats' average positions on affirmative action from 1986 to 2020, conditional on matching the ideological orientation of their party.[24] The center panel tracks their positions on government aid to Blacks, spanning 1972 to 2020.

Like social welfare, polarization on race is circumscribed, confined to partisans in ideological sync with their party. Yet throughout almost the entire time period our data cover, polarization was one-sided. Consider affirmative action (left column). Opposition is massive among Republican identifiers. Strictly speaking, core Republicans are the most opposed. But this is a distinction without a difference. White Republicans, all in all, were and are overwhelmingly opposed to race-based affirmative action in hiring.[25] The telltale key to the

---

[24] We restrict our analysis to non-Hispanic whites for two reasons. First, we posit that the central difference between social welfare and racial attitudes is that white Democrats were on board for social welfare liberalism but not racial liberalism. By looking only at non-Hispanic whites, we can see whether white Democrats that knew and shared their party's ideological orientation indeed saw it this way. Second, non-white Democrats should be more racially liberal than white Democrats, because non-whites have been the beneficiaries of federal efforts to promote racial equality. Indeed, when we examine non-whites' attitudes on affirmative action and government aid to Blacks, we see that core non-white Democrats in 1972 were much more supportive of both race-based affirmative action and government aid to Blacks. Interestingly, however, even non-white Democrats became less liberal on both issues in the intervening years – presumably picking up on some of the backlash we see from white Democrats. Meanwhile, while non-white Republicans have been consistently conservative on affirmative action and generally center-right on government aid to Blacks, low cell counts for non-white Republicans (e.g., *n* only surpasses 100 in 1990) make it difficult to extrapolate.

[25] Skeptical readers might wonder whether white Democrats' reluctance to take their party's side reflects more uncertainty about the Democratic Party's position on racial issues in the aftermath of the Southern Realignment. According to Hill and Tausonovitch (2017), however, ideological

The Political Dynamics of Partisan Polarization 29

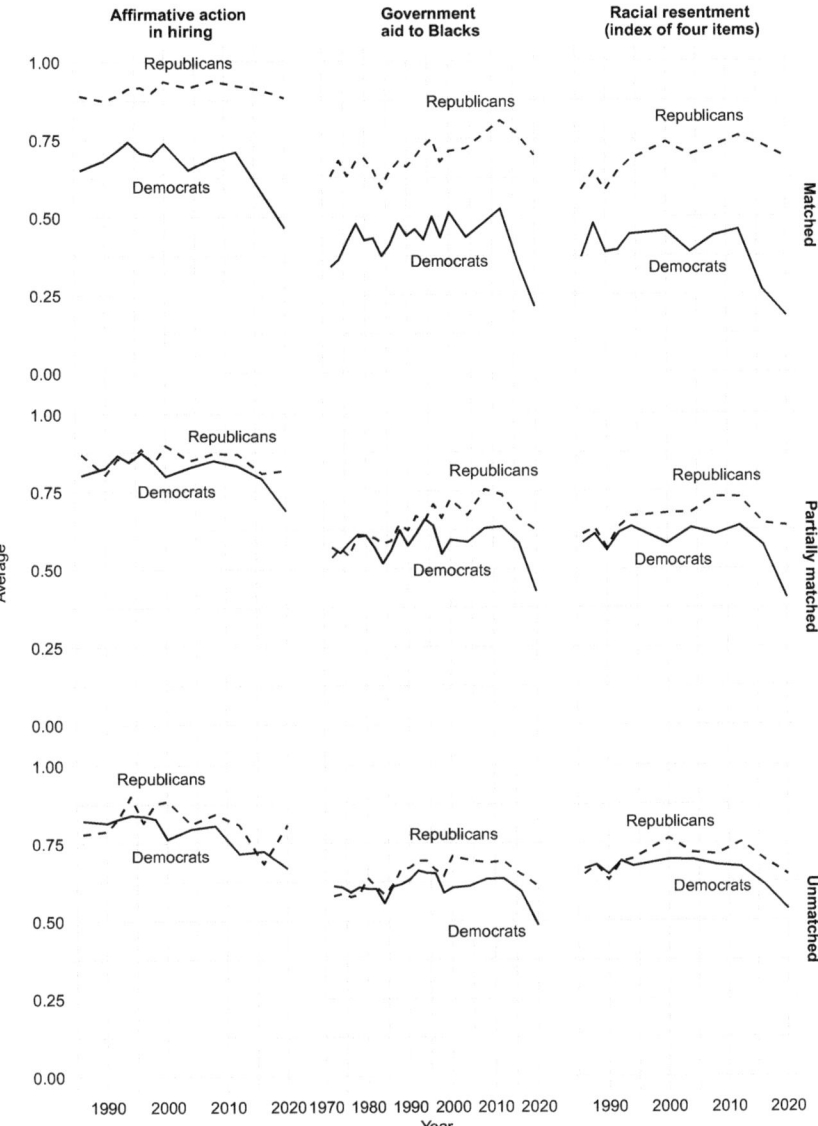

Figure 10 Whites' attitudes on racial politics, 1972–2020, by partisanship and matching status. Higher scores indicate more conservative attitudes; all variables rescaled between 0 and 1. Data: ANES cumulative file, white (non-Hispanic) partisan identifiers only.

---

differences between Democratic and Republican primary voters emerged in Southern states *earlier* than in non-Southern states. This suggests that regardless of party ID, those that know and share their party's ideology have long understood that the Republicans are the party of racial conservatism and the Democrats the party of racial liberalism.

politics of affirmative action, however, is that opposition was nearly as strong on the left as on the right; until recently, even core white Democrats were more likely to oppose than support affirmative action. Yes, white Democrats have turned to the left in the last few years. Yet even by 2020, and even for white Democrats who share the ideological orientation of their party, deep divisions on affirmative action remain. In 2020, white Democrats who fully matched their party's ideological orientation were about as likely to oppose as to support affirmative action in hiring.

The ANES question asks about affirmative action in a demanding form – preferential treatment for Blacks.[26] It could be argued that whites' broad opposition to affirmative action – on the political left as well as the right – reflects reactions to a normatively contestable policy that happens to be about race rather than attitudes about racial equality itself. Hence our analysis of attitudes toward government aid to Blacks (middle panel of Figure 10). Here, the policy alternatives parallel the alternatives on the social welfare agenda: The government should help Blacks or Blacks should help themselves.

As the middle panel of Figure 10 shows, white Republicans oppose government aid to Blacks – more so if they are in ideological sync with their party, but distinctly so even if not. And white Democrats? If they do not know and share the ideological orientation of their party, white Democrats have taken the conservative position on government aid to Blacks only slightly less often than Republicans for most of the time series. Perhaps a surprise, perhaps not. What is a surprise, to us certainly, are the attitudes of *core* white Democrats – that is, Democrats who know theirs is the liberal party, identify as liberal, and take liberal positions on social welfare (see Figure 7). Core white Democrats were effectively *neutral* on government aid to Blacks for most of the time series, showing only a tepid preference for their party's position. Only in 2016 did they clearly rally to their party's side. Core white Democrats' support for government aid to Blacks is currently as strong as core white Republicans' opposition, while white Democrats who do not fully match their party's ideology have moved from opposing government aid to Blacks to taking a neutral position.

---

[26] With follow-up questions asking about strength of support and opposition, the ANES question on affirmative action reads as follows: "Some people say that because of past discrimination blacks should be given preference in hiring and promotion. Others say that such preference in hiring and promotion of blacks is wrong because it gives blacks advantages they haven't earned. What about your opinion – are you for or against preferential hiring and promotion of blacks?" Note that unlike the question on government aid to Blacks, the question on affirmative action lacks a neutral midpoint. If core white Democrats had been able (in 2016 and 2020) to register a *neutral* position on affirmative action, we suspect their about-face on the issue would look less dramatic.

We cannot pinpoint the complex of events triggering core white Democrats' mobilization on issues of race. Was it a reaction to the May 2020 murder of George Floyd and other unarmed Blacks killed by police? Does it reflect a backlash to the Trumpian turn in politics? Or some combination of the two (or some third or fourth factor)? With the data at hand, we cannot tell. We can provide assurance that these results reflect more than a fluke choice of two questions.

The right column of Figure 10 reports trends in "racial resentment," an amalgam of animus against Blacks and liberalism-conservatism.[27] Higher scores on the racial resentment index indicate stronger support for the Republican Party's interpretation of racial conservatism; lower scores indicate stronger support for the Democratic Party's interpretation of racial liberalism. Judged by this measure, core white Democrats became more liberal on racial politics only after 2010 – joined to a more muted degree by white Democrats not ideologically in sync with the Democratic Party.

2.3.2 Polarization as Party Cohesion

The more cohesive a party in the electorate, the greater the latitude of the party in government to polarize without losing the backing of its core supporters. Party cohesion is a joint product – the proportion of the party's supporters who are both core supporters (knowing and sharing the ideological orientation of their party) *and* who align with the party on a particular issue or belief.

Still focusing on non-Hispanic whites, Figure 11 tracks levels of party cohesion on racial issues, from the earliest available data points through 2020, for core Republicans and core Democrats. On racial politics, the Republican Party has had two advantages. First, it enjoys a larger proportion of supporters who share its ideological orientation. Second, throughout far and away most of this period, the racial policies and philosophy of the Republican Party appealed to both white Republicans and substantial numbers of white Democrats. Thanks to both these advantages, white Republicans have been decisively more cohesive than white Democrats on both racial policies and indicators of racial resentment – often two times or more as cohesive. It is all the more striking, therefore, that the difference between core supporters of the two parties disappears by 2020 on all but affirmative action. Whether this is enduring or transitory, time will tell.

---

[27] What "racial resentment" measures is the subject of a long-standing controversy. At present, it is generally agreed that it measures racial liberalism-conservatism, with the proviso that it is not agreed what exactly racial liberalism-conservatism is.

Figure 11 Party cohesion on racial attitudes: matched and issue-sorted whites in the party coalitions, 1972–2020. The plots show the proportions of white (non-Hispanic) Republican and Democratic identifiers that both matched their party's ideological orientation and shared their party's position on each attitude. Data: ANES cumulative file, white (non-Hispanic) partisan identifiers only.

There is a tendency, most often in popular commentary but not uncommon in political science analyses, to bifurcate the politics of race. Either one is for racial equality and therefore should support policies whose intent is to achieve it however they propose to do it, or one opposes racial equality. The political point of Figure 11 is that, from the perspective of white Democrats, there is a world of difference between affirmative action and social welfare spending to improve the social and economic standing of Blacks. Core white Democrats are now on board with a liberal program on race. They are not on board with a progressive one.

2.4 Cultural Politics

The politics of social welfare conforms to the popular picture of polarization as symmetrical; the politics of race has been emphatically asymmetrical until just the last few years. Cultural politics is a hybrid.

2.4.1 Two Levels Again

Conflicts between the parties are our concern, and clashes over cultural issues are front and center now. There is all the more reason, therefore, to point out an emerging consensus that cuts against the "culture war" narrative: increased tolerance toward gays and lesbians.[28]

Figure 12 tracks trends, from 1988 to 2020, for three indicators of acceptance toward gays and lesbians – support for adoption by same-sex couples, support for laws protecting gay people from discrimination in hiring, and support for gays in the military.[29] The y-axis is scaled such that lower scores indicate more traditional positions on gay rights.

The trends for all three indicators are the same, albeit more pronounced for the issue of adoption by same-sex couples. Republicans and Democrats, whether in ideological sync with their party or not, have become more tolerant toward gays – readier to support same-sex couples' right to adopt, readier to protect gays from discrimination in hiring, and readier to support allowing gays to serve openly in the military. To be sure, core Republicans have more holdouts than their Democratic counterparts, but they have become more accepting of gays at the same rate as others, albeit still less so at every point throughout the time series. Some aspects of cultural politics are encouraging.[30]

---

[28] We are encouraged to present these results thanks to the more fulsome demonstration of cultural shift by Atkinson et al. (2021). Our additional contribution is to make explicit the parallel trends of Republicans and Democrats.

[29] The ANES item about gays in the military only runs through 2012.

[30] While tolerance toward LGBTQ+ people has undoubtedly increased, public opinion research offers additional interpretations of the cross-currents responsible for this secular trend. What we call "cross-currents" might better reflect the jumble of policy preferences characteristic of some self-styled "moderates" (see Broockman 2016; Fowler et al. 2023). For our purposes, what matters is that these cross-pressures are not sufficiently patterned that they could manifest as

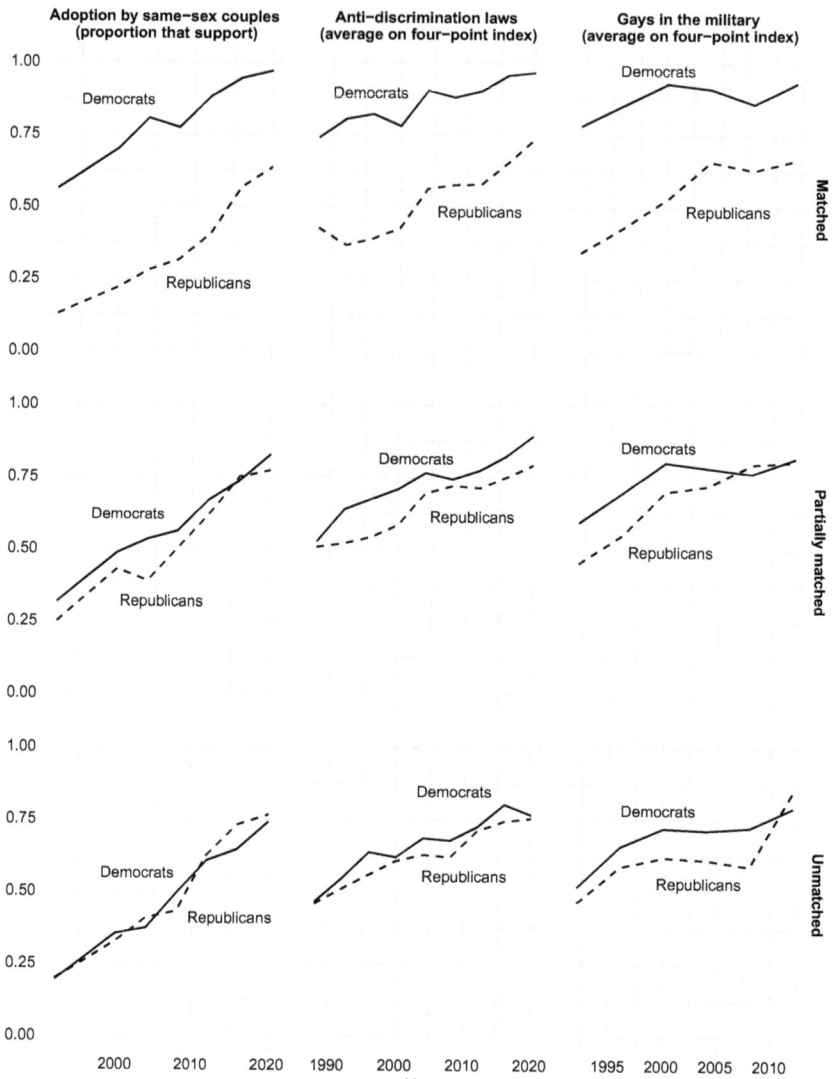

Figure 12 Tolerance toward gays and lesbians, 1988–2020, by partisanship and matching status. All measures were rescaled so that higher scores indicate more progressive attitudes. Data: ANES cumulative file, partisan identifiers only.

Nevertheless, Figure 12 drives home the limitations of over-time ANES analyses by what it does not show. The goal is to track change over an extended period of time, which means tracking responses to questions repeated over this

---

"new" ideological dimensions. We are indebted to Christopher Hare for bringing this point to our attention.

period of time. But cultural politics is quicksilver politics. As agreement emerges on one front, a firestorm erupts on another. Gay rights were once the battlefield. The rights of transgender people – tapping different concerns and policies – are frontline warfare now. How they will be resolved, if they will be resolved, is beyond our reach. Our best prediction, based on the dynamics of cultural politics we have tracked, is that whether or not they are resolved, a firestorm will erupt on yet another front of cultural politics.

2.4.2 Polarization as Policy Divergence

Thus far, our mission has been to track the trajectories of partisan conflict over an extended period, ideally from well before polarization accelerated in the 1990s and 2000s, in any event over the longest period practical. The ANES is designed to do just this. However, some of the issues most intensely contested at the present moment – the rights of transgender people, gender-affirming care for transgender children, and censorship of teaching materials related to sexuality and gender identity – are too recent to illuminate the longer-run dynamics of polarization on cultural issues. Unfortunately, there is not a dearth of divisive issues to study. Abortion and gun control are two important culture-war issues, each the subject of repeated survey questions on multiple ANES cycles. Moreover, the ANES has assessed moral traditionalism,[31] a broader measure of cultural conservatism-liberalism, in many election cycles since 1986. For all three of these measures, Figure 13 shows partisan divergence, conditional on party supporters' orienting themselves to match their party's orientation.

Figure 13 shows that policy divergence on abortion has been circumscribed, restricted to core supporters. Yet while the parties' core supporters diverged at approximately the same time and pace, core Republicans' attitudes experienced a more dramatic change. Between 1980 and 2020, core Democrats became more stridently pro-choice, doubling down on their party's position. But core Republicans crossed the ideological divide – beginning the time series with more pro-choice attitudes and gravitating toward anti-abortion positions. Meanwhile, the positions of Democrats and Republicans whose ideological orientations do not match their parties' overlap one another – indeed, for all practical purposes do not change for the majority of this period. Only the positions of core Democrats and core Republicans diverged – and diverged they did.

---

[31] To be sure, moral traditionalism taps more abstract values than abortion, gun control, and other social issues. However, while moral traditionalism is not a policy issue (per se), both parties use symbolic language to describe their respective orientations on "culture war" debates (Leege et al. 2002). Moral traditionalism thus reflects a domain-specific way to measure whether partisans have accepted their parties' cultural attitudes (see also Goren, Federico, and Kittilson 2013).

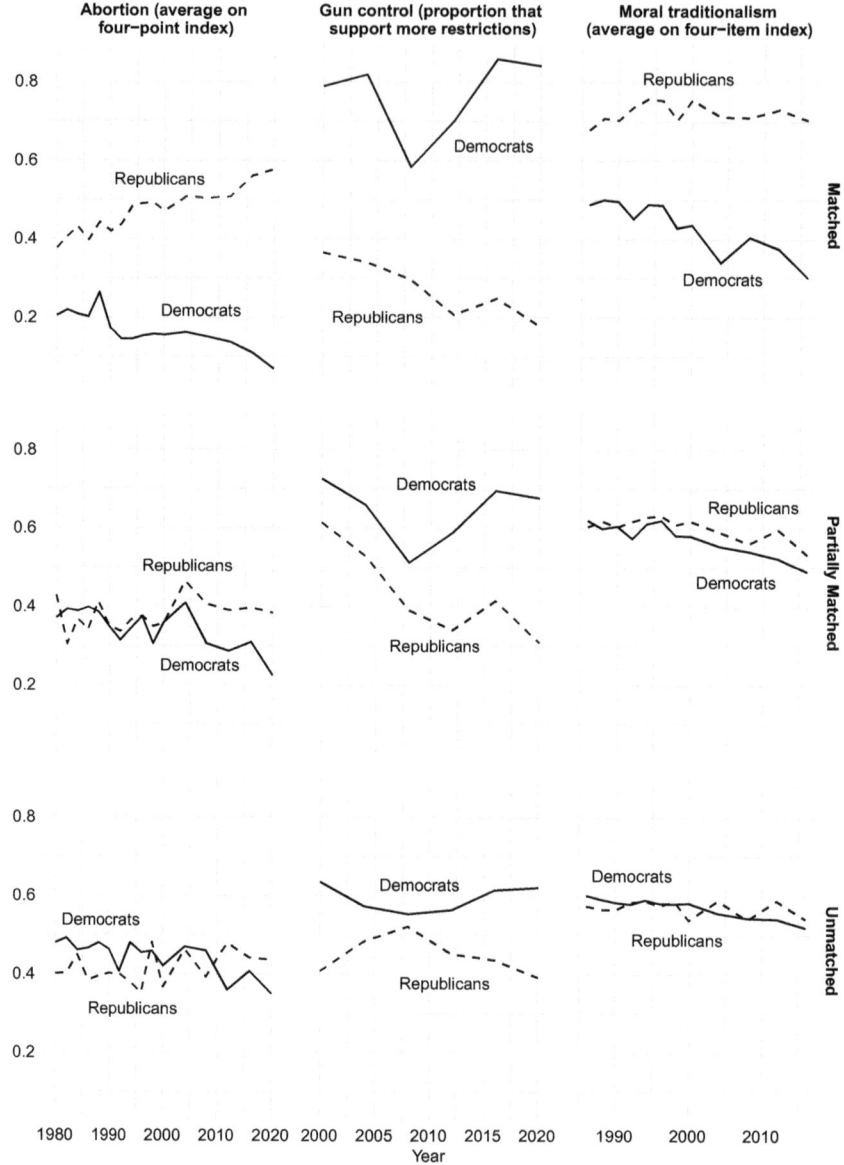

Figure 13 Attitudes on cultural issues, 1980–2020, by partisanship and matching status. Continuous variables were rescaled between 0 and 1; higher scores indicate more conservative attitudes. Data: ANES cumulative file, partisan identifiers only.

By contrast, the dynamics of gun control attitudes are erratic. From 2000 to 2020, core Republicans became markedly less likely to support making gun purchases more difficult, opting instead to support keeping the rules the same – not an entirely unambiguous position given that gun purchases were made easier over these years.[32] The trend for Democrats is more nearly a rollercoaster. Between 2004 and 2008, the percentage of core Democrats who wanted to make gun access more difficult dropped from 81 to 58 percent – only to rebound to 85 percent by 2016. The pattern is similar for Democrats whose ideological orientation partly matches their parties. In 2004, 65 percent favored making gun access more difficult; this fell to 58 percent in 2008, then jumped to 69 percent in 2020. Why the seesaw pattern? Why, more particularly, the slide in support in the first decade? Why indeed? The year 2004 saw the expiration of the Federal Assault Weapons Ban, 2007 the massacre at Virginia Tech (at the time the deadliest mass shooting in U.S. history), and 2012 the Sandy Hook massacre in Newtown, Connecticut. Here as elsewhere, caution is the order of the day. The time series is short. The results are subject to sampling and measurement error. The lesson: The best data are not always good enough.[33]

The partisan divide over abstract values (e.g., "The world is always changing and we should adjust our view of moral behavior to account for these changes") is instructive. Moral traditionalism has been cast as a "policy principle" (Goren 2013) that helps voters develop more concrete policy attitudes. However, neither party publishes a catechism of abstract doctrinal statements on morals. If matched partisans have polarized on the abstract values that undergird culture-war debates, this speaks to their having learned what it *means* to share their party's orientation on cultural politics. As Leege et al. (2002) demonstrate, the partisan significance of "culture war" politics involves both programmatic positions and a symbolic vocabulary for mobilizing voters. Thus, people who know and share their party's ideology should learn not just what policy *positions* go together, but also how their party talks about and justifies these positions. The right column of Figure 13 accordingly presents the over-time trends for moral traditionalism, an index based on four questions dealing with cultural values and norms; the trend line runs from 1986 to 2016, the last year that all four moral traditionalism items appeared on the ANES.[34] Much like the

---

[32] In 2004, the U.S. Congress let expire the Federal Assault Weapons Ban. For its part, the U.S. Supreme Court recognized (for the first time) an *individual* constitutional right to possess a firearm for self-defense in the home (*D.C. v. Heller,* 2008), incorporating this right at the state level shortly thereafter (*McDonald v. Chicago,* 2010).

[33] For a telling analysis demonstrating more marked sorting on gun ownership among Republicans using Pew Research Center data, see Fiorina (2017, figure 3.5, 56).

[34] The moral traditionalism index represents an additive summary of responses to four items: "The world is always changing and we should adjust our view of moral behavior to account for these changes" (reverse-coded for directionality); "People should be allowed to live according to their own moral standards even if these are very different from our own" (reverse-coded for directionality); "This country would have many fewer problems if there were more emphasis on traditional family ties"; and "The newer lifestyles are contributing to the breakdown of society." Response options for each item ranged from "strongly agree" to "strongly disagree," with

abortion issue, polarization on moral traditionalism is confined to partisans in ideological sync with their party. Similar to racial politics, however, we find a polarization lag favoring the right. Core Republicans were polarized earlier and more comprehensively on questions of moral traditionalism. Core Democrats polarized later and more gradually – only becoming as liberal by 2010 as core Republicans were in the early 1990s.

2.4.3 Polarization as Party Cohesion

Party cohesion indexes the size of the bloc of core supporters who take their party's side on an issue their party actively contests. Substantive issues matter selectively (witness core white Democrats' reluctance to stand with their party on issues of race). But party matters extensively thanks to the higher proportion of core supporters in the Republican coalition. Systematic asymmetry in party cohesion is the expected result.

Our examination of cohesion on cultural attitudes demonstrates this trend yet again. Figure 14 maps party cohesion scores from 1980 for abortion, from 2000 for gun control, and from 1986 for each item in the moral traditionalism index.

On abortion, the parties became increasingly cohesive at roughly the same rate after 2000 and are comparably cohesive at present. In contrast, although both parties became more cohesive on gun control after 2000, Republicans are significantly more like-minded, thanks to the greater number of their supporters who know and share the ideological orientation of their party. To assess the consistency of the trends over time for cultural conservatism-liberalism, we estimate separate party cohesion scores for each item in the moral traditionalism index. As the trends for three of the four items make plain, although both parties became more cohesive after 2000, core Republicans have outpaced their Democratic counterparts here too. In sum, with the notable exception of abortion, core Republicans are decisively more cohesive than core Democrats on cultural issues.

2.5 Domain Constraint

The master theme of research on partisan polarization has been symmetry – regular Republicans and Democrats lining up with their parties at roughly the same rate and pace, perhaps not with equal diligence but markedly just the same. Asymmetry, in contrast, is our motif.

To throw a spotlight on asymmetries in convergence across domains, we look at three issues, each representing a different policy domain: government-guaranteed

---

"neither agree nor disagree" a neutral midpoint. Responses of "don't know" were coded at the midpoint.

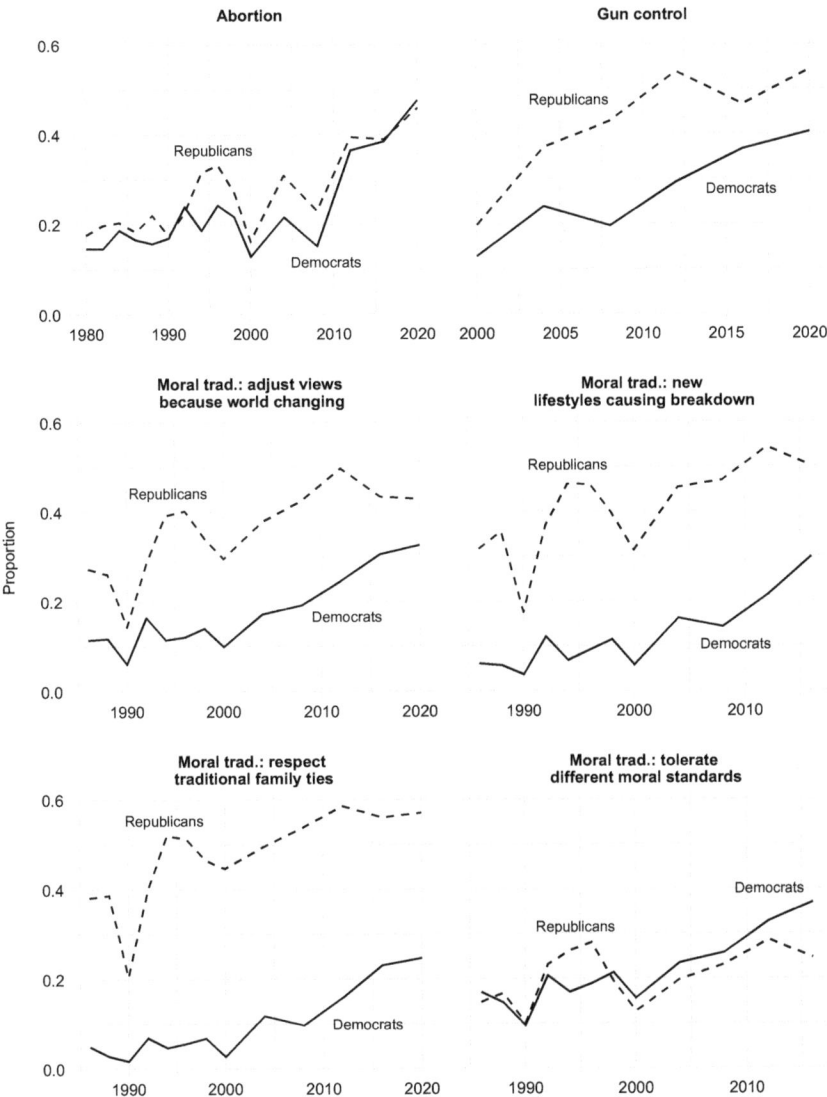

Figure 14 Party cohesion on cultural attitudes: matched and issue-sorted partisans in the party coalitions, 1980–2020. The plots show the proportions of Republican and Democratic identifiers that both matched their party's ideological orientation and shared their party's position on each attitude. Data: ANES cumulative file, partisan identifiers only.

jobs, abortion, and government aid to Blacks. Of the available ANES items from each domain, these have appeared most consistently; the item on abortion first appeared in 1980, the others in 1972. Figure 15 reports the levels of constraint

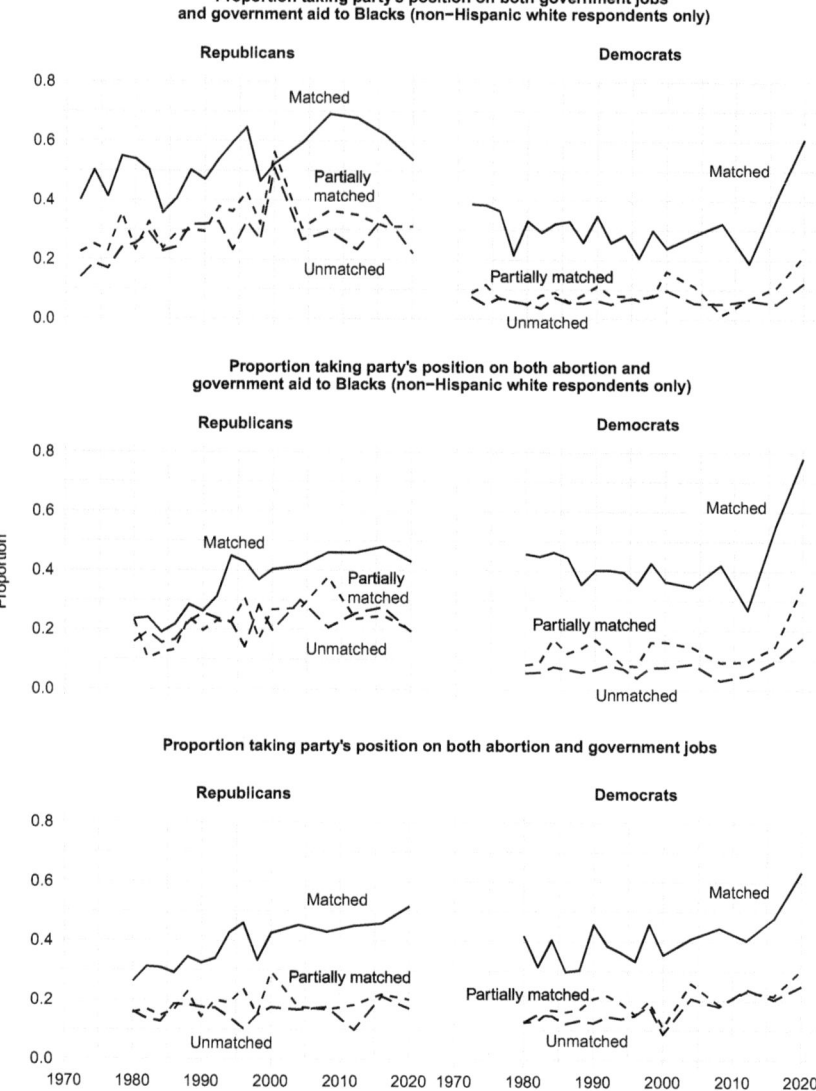

Figure 15 Partisan identifiers' issue constraint, 1972–2020, by matching status. Data: ANES cumulative file, partisan identifiers only.

across policy domains, conditional on the degree of matching, over the last half-century or so.

Again we see a picture of two publics. For Republicans and Democrats who do not know and share the political outlook of their party, it is as though time has not passed and American politics has not polarized. Only a small minority, typically on the order of one in five, take similarly conservative or liberal positions on issues in different domains. Like policy divergence, constraint is centered on – indeed, for all practical purposes confined to – core supporters of the two parties.

Polarization lag was the signature feature of racial politics – with core white Republicans lining up with their party early, and core white Democrats lining up with their party only very recently. The top row of Figure 15 shows the proportions of white (non-Hispanic) Republicans and Democrats, conditional on matching status, who have taken their party's position on both government activism to boost jobs and government aid to Blacks. Again, the asymmetry between the parties stands out. Among non-Hispanic whites in 1972, roughly the same percentage of core Republicans and core Democrats took their party's position on both issues. However, unlike core white Republicans, core white Democrats saw no appreciable increase in rates of constraint on social welfare and racial issues for most of this period. Only after 2010 did they tie the two together at markedly higher rates, constraint between the two policy domains dramatically shooting up between 2012 and 2020.

The middle row of Figure 15 shows a comparable picture of constraint across cultural and racial politics, from 1980 to 2020, documenting the proportions of white Republicans and Democrats who took their party's positions on both abortion and government aid to Blacks. Here the difference between the two parties takes the opposite form. Between 1980 and 1994, core white Republicans made only a weak connection between the two policy domains. However, as their party made its opposition to abortion more explicit, they became markedly more likely to take consistently conservative positions on both issues. In contrast, throughout this period, roughly 40 percent of core white Democrats connected their views on both abortion and government aid to Blacks. As issues of racial injustice caught fire in 2020 and access to abortion was threatened by then-President Trump's appointment of three conservative justices to the U.S. Supreme Court, an astonishing 78 percent took consistently liberal positions on both issues.

The bottom row of Figure 15 reports the proportion of Republicans and Democrats taking party-consistent stands on abortion and government activism to boost jobs. Core Democrats make stronger connections between the policy domains at the very end of the period – unsurprisingly, given their near-unanimous support for abortion rights in 2020. This detail aside, symmetry is the pattern for constraint on social welfare and cultural issues. Core Democrats and Republicans show similar levels of constraint on abortion and government activism to boost jobs, near as makes no difference.

2.6 Political Convictions: Emotion and Belief

"Affective polarization" is a leading paradigm in studies of partisan polarization (Diermeier and Li 2019; Iyengar and Krupenkin 2018; Iyengar, Sood, and Lelkes 2012; Mason 2018; Mason and Wronski 2018). The nerve of the idea is that to identify with a party is to establish an emotional attachment rooted in a social identity (see also Green, Palmquist, and Schickler 2002). As Iyengar and Westwood (2015) put it, "The sense of group membership inculcates positive evaluations of the ingroup and correspondingly hostile evaluations of outgroups" (690). So it is in life, the reasoning goes, and still more so in politics. Analyzing the consequences of affective polarization, Iyengar and Westwood (2015) conclude that "fear and loathing" drives regular Republicans and Democrats to distrust and discriminate against members of the opposing party – a reflexive emotional response minimally associated with ideas and beliefs.

The issue, to be clear, is not whether party identification *is* an emotional attachment, nor whether hostility toward the opposing party has spiraled up as the parties have polarized further apart. The issue is how far emotions in politics are free-standing, with a life of their own, separate from people's beliefs, preferences, and convictions about what is right and what is wrong, what is morally acceptable and what is morally unacceptable. On an unqualified view of affective polarization, what people believe substantively – what they are concerned about when they fear that the country and their place in it are at risk, what they are adamant that the government has an obligation to do or to refrain from doing – is incidental. What drives the polarization of the parties are raw emotions.

Setting extreme claims aside, a focus on affective polarization calls out the propulsive force of emotion in the polarization of politics, above all, the hostility against and fear of one's political opponents. One counter-claim is that policy convictions, not affect, are the critical element. In a series of ingenious experiments, Orr and colleagues have brought out the pivotal role of substantive commitments as a basis of partisan animosity (Orr and Huber 2020; Orr, Fowler and Huber 2023; see also Costa 2021; Rogowski and Sutherland 2016; Webster and Abramowitz 2017). At the same time, in another deeply thought-through analysis, Dias and Lelkes (2022) offer a counterclaim – that partisan identity ties together both affect and belief. For Dias and Lelkes (2022), issue positions produce partisan animosity because they are "coded" as Republican or Democratic, and thus trigger the same emotional ties that party ID does.

We agree with Orr and Huber (2020) that politics is substantive and with Dias and Lelkes (2022) that partisan identity is pivotal. Where we differ is on the urgency of conceptual parsimony. Both analyses seek to establish the nature of the relationship between affect and belief. For us, two concepts are one too many. For partisans who know what their party stands for and stand with it, affect and belief are bound up together inextricably. As for the concept of partisan identity, we favor Occam's razor here, too. For core supporters who know and share their party's ideology, partisan identity *is* a political identity.

Conceptual parsimony pays. Republicans and Democrats who believe in what their party stands for know what is at stake if the other party wins elections.[35] They have the strongest reasons to "fear and loathe" the other party.[36] For them, the distinction between political belief and feelings about the opposing party evaporates. What could it possibly mean to believe in what your party stands for, to prioritize the goals and values it prioritizes, to be convinced that the other party will take the country in a disastrous direction – and yet be indifferent if it won the election?

On our approach, for those who know what their party stands for and stand with it, the distinction between political beliefs and political feelings is a distinction without a difference, precisely *because* they know what their party stands for and stand with it. But there is a long-standing alternative explanation on the books. According to this alternative account, a politically consequential portion of the electorate, an "engaged public," pays attention to politics, is tolerably well-informed about it, and participates actively in it. They are, runs the reasoning, the most likely to know what the two parties stand for and, as politics polarizes and the parties-in-government move to the ideological poles, therefore the most likely to fear and loathe the opposing party (Abramowitz 2010, 2013).

On the "engaged public" hypothesis, political sophistication – variously understood – is the mechanism binding belief and feeling together. On our account, the mechanism is substantive agreement, the supporters of a party orienting themselves parallel with their party's orientation. The two accounts

---

[35] See Druckman et al. (2024) for an innovative demonstration of the special potency of cues making salient the policy commitments of the opposing party.

[36] Indeed, in the aftermath of the 2024 U.S. presidential election, we challenge any political scientist reading this monograph to consider whether they supported their preferred candidate primarily because they felt an emotional attachment to their party, not because they believed the other party's presidential candidate was dangerous and misguided. For example, suppose that a colleague claims that they voted against Donald Trump because in their view, he posed a danger to democratic norms and institutions. We would never tell such a colleague that they were really motivated by blind loyalty to the Democratic Party or affinity for the social groups in the Democratic coalition. Nor would we say that by dint of their political sophistication, they have learned to rationalize as sincere concern for the country what are essentially non-ideological impulses. To do so would be to deny what politics is about – the emotion that comes with high-stakes decisions.

are not mutually exclusive, obviously enough. However, being politically engaged and informed is the best-tested and longest-standing mechanism of political learning in mass publics (e.g., Converse 1964). A comparison of the importance of the two mechanisms, matching and political sophistication, thus provides a strong test of our theoretical claims.

Accordingly, we use the 1988 and 2020 ANES to model the relationship between partisan affect and partisan belief, conditional on matching and various forms of political sophistication. The analysis covers the three major policy domains. To measure social welfare attitudes, we use an additive index based on respondents' beliefs about government-guaranteed jobs, government services and spending, and government-provided health insurance. To assess cultural values, we use all available items dealing with moral traditionalism; two were present on the 2020 ANES, and four on the 1988 ANES.[37] Finally, our measure of racial conservatism was built from two items, tapping respondents' beliefs about government aid to Blacks and race-based affirmative action in hiring. (Note that our analysis of racial attitudes, here as elsewhere, is confined to non-Hispanic whites.)

For each year and dependent variable, we estimate a sequence of models. Each model includes an interaction between matching and affective polarization. The former is based on a 0–1 scale (0 = unmatched; 0.5 = partially matched; 1 = matched); the latter is the difference in feeling thermometer ratings for the Republican and Democratic parties. Model 1 includes this interaction only. Each subsequent model adds a second interaction term, interacting affective polarization with an alternative measure of political sophistication – political knowledge[38] (Model 2), low-level activism[39]

---

[37] On the 2020 ANES, two moral traditionalism measures appeared on the post-election wave, asking respondents whether "The world is always changing and we should adjust our view of moral behavior to account for these changes" (reverse-coded for directionality) and "This country would have many fewer problems if there were more emphasis on traditional family ties." These items appeared on the 1988 ANES too, along with the two others: "We should be more tolerant of people who choose to live according to their own moral standards, even if these are very different from our own" (reverse-coded for directionality) and "The newer lifestyles are contributing to the breakdown of society." Our measure of moral traditionalism is an additive index of the two (2020) or four (1988) available items. Data are drawn from the individual cross-sections for each year (American National Election Studies 1999, 2021).

[38] On the 2020 ANES, the preelection module asked respondents to identify the party that currently controlled the (1) U.S. House and (2) U.S. Senate; (3) the number of years in a U.S. senator's term-in-office; and (4) the federal program (among four options; correct answer was "foreign aid") on which the federal government spent the least amount of money. In 2020, then, we measured political knowledge based on the number of correct responses to these questions. In 1988, our measure of political knowledge was based only on respondents' knowledge of which party controlled the Senate and House before the November election.

[39] Low-level activism captures the number of (self-reported) campaign activities in which the respondent engaged. More information is available in the online appendix.

(Model 3), interest in politics[40] (Model 4), and educational attainment[41] (Model 5). In this manner, we can test whether other measures of political engagement better account for the relationship between partisan affect and policy attitudes.[42]

For both 1988 and 2020, Tables 1–3 report the results of our models, reporting the effects of affective polarization on social welfare attitudes (Table 1), moral traditionalism (Table 2), and racial attitudes (Table 3). For ease of interpretation, we have rescaled all variables between 0 and 1. The coefficient on partisan affect represents the predicted difference in policy attitudes between the most affectively polarized *unmatched* Democrat and the most affectively polarized *unmatched* Republican – scoring their own party at 100 on the feeling thermometer and the opposing party at zero. The interaction between partisan affect and matching, then, indexes the degree to which matching increases the average marginal effect of affective polarization.

Tables 1–3 have three major takeaways. First, matching matters for consolidating affect and belief, and the significance of matching has increased as polarization has accelerated. Compared to unmatched partisans in 1988, the most affectively polarized *matched* Republican and Democrat diverged an additional 0.33 points on government conservatism, 0.39 points on moral traditionalism, and (for non-Hispanic whites) 0.06 points on racial conservatism; for racial conservatism, the interaction between affective polarization and matching did not reach statistical significance.[43] However, among matched partisans in 2020, this difference in the average marginal effect of affective polarization was about 0.50 points for government conservatism and 0.63 points for moral traditionalism. Unlike 1988, moreover, matching conditioned the effect of affective polarization on non-Hispanic whites' racial attitudes; compared to unmatched partisans, the models predicted an approximately 0.51-point greater divergence between the most affectively polarized *matched*

---

[40] Interest in politics is based on two measures, asking about respondents' interest in that year's presidential campaign (1 = not at all interested; 2 = somewhat interested; and 3 = very interested) and the frequency with which they follow current affairs. In 1988, attention to current affairs was a four-point scale (0 = hardly at all; 1 = only now and then; 2 = some of the time; and 3 = most of the time); in 2020, it was a five-point scale (0 = never; 1 = some of the time; 2 = about half the time; 3 = most of the time; and 4 = always). Each measure received equal weight.

[41] Educational attainment is measured using the standard, six-point scale (0 = less than high-school degree; and 5 = post-graduate degree or higher).

[42] Note that the models estimated are trimmed. The standard miscellany of demographic control variables – age, religious attendance, or racial or ethnic background – are not included. Our objective is political analysis, to clarify the distinguishing politics of partisan polarization. The key, on our reasoning, is matching – party supporters using their parties as models to learn what goes with what, thanks to their knowing and sharing the ideological orientation of their party.

[43] For the interaction between matching and affective polarization, reported effect sizes are averaged across the five models for each year. Especially in 2020, the coefficient on the interaction between matching and affective polarization was remarkably stable across the different specifications.

Table 1 Relationship between social welfare conservatism and partisan affective polarization, conditional on matching and other forms of political sophistication.

	Dependent variable: social welfare conservatism									
	1988 ANES					2020 ANES				
	Model 1	Model 2	Model 3	Model 4	Model 5	Model 1	Model 2	Model 3	Model 4	Model 5
Pro-GOP affect	0.20***	0.11*	0.15***	0.06	0.16***	0.14***	0.07**	0.12***	0.07*	0.10***
	(0.04)	(0.06)	(0.05)	(0.06)	(0.05)	(0.03)	(0.03)	(0.03)	(0.04)	(0.03)
Matching	−0.13***	−0.12***	−0.12***	−0.11***	−0.13***	−0.21***	−0.20***	−0.17***	−0.20***	−0.20***
	(0.03)	(0.03)	(0.03)	(0.04)	(0.03)	(0.02)	(0.02)	(0.02)	(0.02)	(0.02)
Political knowledge		−0.02					−0.03			
		(0.03)					(0.02)			
Low-level activism			−0.11*					−0.14***		
			(0.06)					(0.02)		
Political interest				−0.07					−0.04	
				(0.05)					(0.02)	
Educational attachment					−0.01					−0.03
					(0.04)					(0.02)
Affect x matching	0.36***	0.29***	0.35***	0.31***	0.32***	0.54***	0.49***	0.49***	0.50***	0.50***
	(0.06)	(0.07)	(0.07)	(0.07)	(0.06)	(0.03)	(0.04)	(0.04)	(0.04)	(0.04)

	(1)	(2)	(3)	(4)	(5)	(6)	(7)	(8)	(9)	(10)
Affect x political knowledge	0.18*** (0.06)					0.20*** (0.04)				
Affect x low-level activism		0.25** (0.12)					0.22*** (0.04)			
Affect x political interest			0.24** (0.09)					0.14*** (0.04)		
Affect x education				0.14* (0.08)					0.16*** (0.03)	
Constant	0.39*** (0.02)	0.40*** (0.03)	0.41*** (0.02)	0.43*** (0.03)	0.39*** (0.02)	0.35*** (0.02)	0.36*** (0.02)	0.35*** (0.02)	0.37*** (0.02)	0.35*** (0.02)
N	1,678	1,490	1,490	1,477	1,649	7,081	6,968	6,374	7,080	6,992
Log likelihood	429.31	427.11	408.91	406.52	427.29	621.70	675.75	260.18	641.26	675.08

Standard errors are in parentheses. Data: ANES 1988 and 2020, partisan identifiers only. The dependent variable, *social welfare conservatism*, is an additive index of attitudes on government guaranteed jobs, government services and spending, and government health insurance. All variables were rescaled between 0 and 1. ***$p < 0.01$; **$p < 0.05$; and *$p < 0.10$.

Table 2 Relationship between moral traditionalism and partisan affective polarization, conditional on matching and other forms of political sophistication.

	Dependent variable: moral traditionalism									
	1988 ANES					2020 ANES				
	Model 1	Model 2	Model 3	Model 4	Model 5	Model 1	Model 2	Model 3	Model 4	Model 5
Pro-GOP affect	−0.04 (0.04)	−0.04 (0.05)	−0.06 (0.04)	−0.03 (0.06)	−0.06 (0.04)	−0.05 (0.03)	−0.11*** (0.04)	−0.07** (0.03)	−0.10** (0.04)	−0.07* (0.04)
Matching	−0.16*** (0.03)	−0.17*** (0.03)	−0.16*** (0.03)	−0.17*** (0.03)	−0.15*** (0.04)	−0.32*** (0.02)	−0.30*** (0.02)	−0.29*** (0.02)	−0.32*** (0.02)	−0.30*** (0.02)
Political knowledge		0.03 (0.03)					−0.06** (0.03)			
Low-level activism			−0.04 (0.06)					−0.12*** (0.03)		
Political interest				0.06 (0.05)					0.02 (0.03)	
Educational attachment					−0.05 (0.05)					−0.04 (0.03)
Affect x matching	0.40*** (0.06)	0.38*** (0.06)	0.38*** (0.06)	0.39*** (0.06)	0.38*** (0.06)	0.67*** (0.04)	0.62*** (0.04)	0.61*** (0.04)	0.64*** (0.04)	0.63*** (0.04)

	ANES 1988					ANES 2020				
Affect x political knowledge		0.01					0.17***			
		(0.06)					(0.05)			
Affect x low-level activism			0.21*					0.29***		
			(0.12)					(0.05)		
Affect x political interest				0.01					0.11***	
				(0.10)					(0.05)	
Affect x education					0.09					0.10**
					(0.09)					(0.05)
Constant	0.61***	0.59***	0.61***	0.57***	0.62***	0.56***	0.58***	0.57***	0.57***	0.55***
	(0.02)	(0.02)	(0.02)	(0.03)	(0.02)	(0.02)	(0.02)	(0.02)	(0.02)	(0.02)
N	1,488	1,488	1,488	1,474	1,463	6,341	6,278	6,341	6,340	6,258
Log likelihood	318.13	322.21	322.98	321.90	311.96	−640.40	−611.75	−609.90	−605.17	−607.18

Standard errors are in parentheses. Data: ANES 1988 and 2020, partisan identifiers only. The dependent variable, *moral traditionalism*, is an additive index based on items available in each year; see the online appendix for details. All variables were rescaled between 0 and 1. ***$p < 0.01$; **$p < 0.05$; and *$p < 0.10$.

Table 3 Relationship between racial conservatism and partisan affective polarization, conditional on matching and other forms of political sophistication.

	Dependent variable: racial conservatism									
	1988 ANES					2020 ANES				
	Model 1	Model 2	Model 3	Model 4	Model 5	Model 1	Model 2	Model 3	Model 4	Model 5
Pro-GOP affect	0.07	0.05	0.06	−0.02	0.04	0.11**	0.03	0.09	0.02	0.002
	(0.05)	(0.06)	(0.06)	(0.08)	(0.06)	(0.05)	(0.06)	(0.05)	(0.07)	(0.06)
Matching	−0.04	−0.03	−0.03	−0.01	−0.002	−0.38***	−0.35***	−0.32***	−0.35***	−0.32***
	(0.04)	(0.04)	(0.04)	(0.05)	(0.05)	(0.04)	(0.04)	(0.04)	(0.04)	(0.04)
Political knowledge		−0.02					−0.15***			
		(0.04)					(0.04)			
Low-level activism			−0.07					−0.25***		
			(0.08)					(0.04)		
Political interest				−0.10					−0.13***	
				(0.07)					(0.04)	
Educational attachment					−0.10					−0.23***
					(0.06)					(0.04)
Affect x matching	0.08	0.07	0.08	0.03	0.03	0.56***	0.51***	0.49***	0.52***	0.46***
	(0.07)	(0.08)	(0.08)	(0.08)	(0.08)	(0.06)	(0.06)	(0.06)	(0.06)	(0.06)

	(1)	(2)	(3)	(4)	(5)	(6)	(7)	(8)	(9)	(10)
Affect x political knowledge		0.04 (0.08)					0.19*** (0.06)			
Affect x low-level activism			0.08 (0.14)					0.27*** (0.07)		
Affect x political interest				0.19* (0.12)					0.16** (0.07)	
Affect x education					0.17 (0.11)					0.33*** (0.06)
Constant	0.68*** (0.03)	0.69*** (0.04)	0.68*** (0.03)	0.73*** (0.04)	0.69*** (0.03)	0.61*** (0.03)	0.68*** (0.03)	0.63*** (0.03)	0.68*** (0.04)	0.69*** (0.03)
N	1,110	1,110	1,110	1,101	1,093	4,632	4,596	4,632	4,631	4,575
Log likelihood	320.68	320.83	321.51	323.29	316.37	−613.44	−589.17	−567.99	−601.94	−535.61

Standard errors are in parentheses. Data: ANES 1988 and 2020, white (non-Hispanic) partisan identifiers only. The dependent variable, *racial conservatism*, is an additive index based on attitudes about (1) race-based affirmative action in hiring and (2) government aid to Blacks. All variables were rescaled between 0 and 1. ***$p < 0.01$; **$p < 0.05$; and *$p < 0.10$.

Republican and Democrat. Note that since we have rescaled our variables between 0 and 1, the effects represent *at least half the scales* for our measures of policy attitudes – the difference between objectively liberal and objectively conservative positions. For linking partisan affect with policy attitudes, matching mattered in 1988 and mattered even more in 2020.

Second, other forms of political sophistication also help partisan identifiers link affect and belief. However, effect sizes differ dramatically depending on policy dimension, metric, and year. In the models of social welfare attitudes, the interaction between affective polarization and each measure of sophistication achieved statistical significance in both 1988 and 2020. Effect sizes were comparable across the two elections. Yet, in the 1988 models of moral traditionalism and racial attitudes, alternate measures of sophistication generally failed to condition the effects of affective polarization. In the 1988 models of racial attitudes, only interest in politics achieved statistical significance when interacted with affective polarization; in the 1988 models of cultural attitudes, only low-level activism conditioned the effects of affective polarization to a statistically significant degree. In 2020, however, all four interaction terms reached statistical significance – conditioning the effects of affective polarization on both moral traditionalism and racial attitudes.

Third, and most critically, the effects of matching are markedly more pronounced than the effects of the standard measures of political sophistication. Across the models using the 2020 ANES, the interaction between matching and affective polarization consistently produced larger coefficients than the interaction between affective polarization and other measures. Moreover, the competing interactions did not dampen the interaction between affective polarization and matching to any meaningful extent. Looking just at 2020, the interaction between affective polarization and matching registered coefficients between 0.49–0.54 for the models of social welfare attitudes, 0.61–0.67 for the models of moral traditionalism, and 0.46–0.56 for the models of racial attitudes. Thus, Abramowitz (2013) is correct to point out that an engaged public *exists*, and that political engagement has some relationship to polarization. But as the mechanism linking affect and belief, traditional measures of political engagement do not hold a candle to matching. Knowing and sharing your party's ideological orientation has far and away the strongest role to play.

At every point, the results show that matching is the primary mechanism binding belief and affect. The striking increase in the number of ideologically aware and committed partisans is the root of the affective polarization of party politics in the United States.

2.7 Policy Extremism

The parties-in-government have pushed policies toward the poles, raising legitimate concerns about extremism (e.g., Mann and Ornstein 2012). This divergence between the parties-in-government, it naturally seems, carries with it the risk that regular Republicans and Democrats will similarly propel themselves to the ideological poles. After all, our analyses have shown that while polarization is confined to partisans whose ideological orientation matches their party's, majorities in both parties now fit this description.

To address this question, Figure 16 assesses whether matched Democrats (on the left) and matched Republicans (on the right) became more extreme between 1984 and 2020. The top panel looks at ideological identification, the dashed line mapping responses in 1984, and the solid black line mapping responses in 2020. What would we see if core supporters became more extremist? Obviously enough, markedly more core Democrats should identify as "extremely liberal," and markedly more core Republicans should identify as "extremely conservative." Yet this is not what we see. Rather, the biggest difference between 2020 and 1984 is that the modal core Democrat now calls herself "liberal" rather than "slightly liberal," while a simple majority of core Republicans now call themselves "conservative." Needless to say, it makes perfect sense that for those practicing ideological partisanship in 2020, the qualifying term *slightly* no longer seems as necessary.

The second panel compares the positions of core Democrats and Republicans on the flagship measure of social welfare politics – attitudes toward government-guaranteed jobs. Specifically, respondents are asked to locate their positions on a seven-point scale, bounded at one end by the position that "The government should see to it that everyone has a good job and good standard of living" and at the other, by the position that "The government should let each person get ahead on their own." Compared to 1984, more core Democrats in 2020 take the most liberal position possible, and more core Republicans take the most conservative position possible. The third panel shows a similar pattern for non-Hispanic whites' positions on government aid to Blacks, where core Democrats – given their late-in-the-day support for racial liberalism – veer particularly sharply to the left. Abortion attitudes, in the bottom panel, show the same result too, with core Democrats more liberal in 2020 compared to 1984, and core Republicans more conservative.

The challenge is what to make of the differences between 1984 and 2020. Politics is heated now, more strongly agree and strongly disagree. But intensity is not extremity. What matters is just what people are advocating or opposing. As Figure 16 shows, core Democrats' modal position on abortion in 2020 was

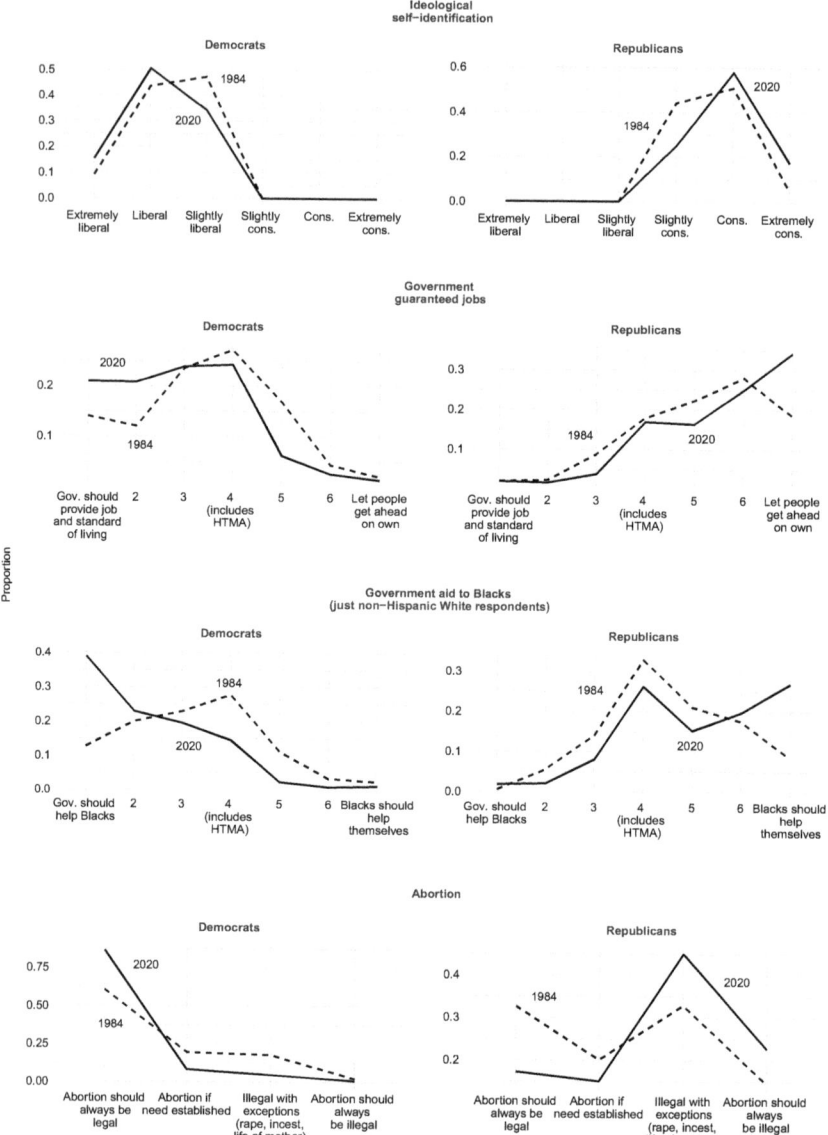

Figure 16 Matched partisans in 1984 and 2020: distributions of ideological self-identification and domain-specific issue positions. HTMA indicates "haven't thought much about this." Data: ANES cumulative file, matched partisan identifiers from the 1984 and 2020 cross-sections.

that women should always have the right to choose whether to have an abortion. It is completely understandable if a person committed to the pro-life movement regards that as an extreme position; but in a contemporary liberal democracy like the United States, it most certainly is not the position of an extremist. For core Republicans in 2020, the modal position was that "abortion should be prohibited except in cases of rape, incest, or danger to the mother's life" – a position strongly rejected by reproductive rights activists, but in a country in which freedom of religion is the first freedom enunciated in the First Amendment, not the position of an extremist either. As for racial politics, it is hardly radical to believe strongly that the government should "make every effort to improve the social and economic position of Blacks." On the other hand, opposition to government aid to Blacks, in and of itself, is no more extreme than opposition to government subsidies for farmers. To make the point more generally, by design, the alternatives that the ANES poses for respondents are not extreme. The questions assess only how strongly respondents favor one or the other approach.[44] But however strongly respondents favor one alternative or the other, purely as a logical matter, they cannot take an extreme position when the alternatives they must choose between are not extreme.

2.8 Matching and Voting Behavior

2.8.1 Polarization and Primary Turnout

Thus far, polarization of the parties-in-the-electorate has been conceptualized as mainly a top-down process. The Republican and Democratic parties-in-government started the process, pushing their policies to their respective ideological poles. Their core supporters – people who know and share their party's ideological orientation – polarized in turn, not to the same degree as the parties-in-government, but significantly all the same. Democrats and Republicans who know what their party stands for and stand with it are committed partisans. They know what is at stake. They act on their beliefs. And given the logic of spatial voting, in a polarized politics, their preferred candidate will be their party's candidate even if his or her positions become extreme and theirs do not.

Just so far as this is so, whether a party's core supporters act on their beliefs is pivotal. Consider primary elections, which have historically lower turnout than general elections. Core supporters, who stand with their party and know what is at stake, should have a stronger incentive to participate in low-stimulus elections compared to fellow partisans with only an emotional attachment to their party. This means that as the parties' core supporters become more consequential in

---

[44] To be sure, some ANES items have wording that overreaches. For example, the item on guaranteed government jobs, one of the longest-running seven-point scales on the ANES, asks whether "the government should see to it that everyone has a job and a good standard of living" or whether "the government should let each person get ahead on his/her own."

primary elections, more ideologically extreme candidates should have a greater advantage. The data at hand allow a partial test of this reasoning.

The left column of Table 4 records rates of matching among partisan identifiers that reported voting in their state's presidential primaries or caucuses (for years with available ANES data) and the general election. Before 2000, core supporters made up a minority of voters in presidential primaries and caucuses – on average, just over one-third. In 2008, the first election after 1992 for which ANES data are available, core supporters made up 56 percent of the electorate in primaries and caucuses. Their share has progressively increased, totaling 67 percent in 2020.

Consistent with the sharp uptick in partisan matching after 2000, matched partisans now compose the majority of partisan voters at both stages of the electoral process. The right column of Table 4 shows a parallel trend for the general election, with core supporters making up an increasingly larger share of the electorate. To be sure, core supporters' share of the primary electorate is usually slightly larger than their share of voters in the general election. The politically consequential point, however, is that they are now the largest share of

Table 4 Self-reported turnout data, 1972–2020: proportion of matched partisans among partisans who reported voting in the presidential primaries and general election.

Percentage of matched partisans among partisan voters in the electorate, 1972–2020

Year	Presidential primaries and caucuses	General election
1972	0.36	0.32
1976	0.39	0.35
1980	0.35	0.36
1984	Not available	0.39
1988	0.37	0.39
1992	0.41	0.42
1996	Not available	0.47
2000	Not available	0.42
2004	Not available	0.49
2008	0.56	0.51
2012	0.63	0.58
2016	0.65	0.59
2020	0.67	0.63

Source: ANES cumulative file (2022), partisan identifiers only. Self-reported turnout data.

the partisan vote in both low and high-stimulus elections. The logic of spatial voting is strict: Parties can nominate more extreme candidates without losing the support of their moderate supporters.

2.8.2 Partisan Asymmetries Bottom-Up

On our account, framework matching is the mechanism regulating the polarization of the parties-in-the-electorate. Consistent with this claim, the proportion of Republicans and Democrats who know and share the ideological framework of their party has increased in tandem with elite polarization. Just as significant politically, however, Republicans are markedly more likely than Democrats to know and share the ideological framework of their party (Figure 8) – at every point in time. It follows straightforwardly that core Republicans will play a larger electoral role than core Democrats.

Table 5 confirms this prediction, reporting rates of matching for Republican and Democratic voters separately. The differences are dramatic. By 1976, matched Republicans composed more than half of the Republicans who self-reported voting in the presidential primaries; by 1980, they composed more than half of Republican general-election voters. By 2020, their share of the Republican electorate had skyrocketed; matched Republicans composed 72 and 77 percent of self-reported voters in the general election and presidential primaries, respectively.

In contrast, it was not until 2016, perhaps under the pressure of Donald Trump's first campaign, that matched Democrats made up a majority of Democratic identifiers in either the presidential primaries or the general election. Even then, matched Republicans' share of their party's voters was 20 percentage points higher in the general election and 23 points higher in the presidential primaries. Simply put, the Republican electorate has a larger ideological core than the Democratic electorate.

As always, caution is called for. Survey respondents often claim to have voted when they did not. The more marginal their ties to a party, it is fair to expect, the more likely they are to be false positives, falsely reporting (perhaps due to social desirability bias) that they turned out to vote. With voter-validated data from the Cooperative Congressional Election Study (CCES, now CES), we can obtain more accurate assessments of matched partisans' shares of the electorate.

6 examines the proportion of matched partisans among primary and election voters in 2016 and 2020, both in the aggregate and broken partisanship. For all intents and purposes, core Republicans' domin- presidential primaries is complete. Among Republicans who voted

Table 5 Self-reported turnout data, 1972–2020, by partisanship: proportion of matched partisans among partisans who reported voting in the presidential primaries and general election.

Proportion matched among partisan voters (self-reported) in the presidential primaries and general election, by partisanship

Year	Presidential primaries and caucuses		General election	
	Republican identifiers	Democratic identifiers	Republican identifiers	Democratic identifiers
1972	0.46	0.28	0.41	0.24
1976	0.51	0.30	0.47	0.25
1980	0.54	0.22	0.51	0.24
1984	Not available	Not available	0.50	0.29
1988	0.55	0.23	0.54	0.25
1992	0.53	0.33	0.52	0.33
1996	Not available	Not available	0.67	0.31
2000	Not available	Not available	0.59	0.29
2004	Not available	Not available	0.63	0.35
2008	0.75	0.44	0.67	0.39
2012	0.78	0.46	0.73	0.45
2016	0.77	0.54	0.70	0.50
2020	0.77	0.59	0.72	0.55

Source: ANES cumulative file (2022), partisan identifiers only. Self-reported turnout data.

in the 2016 and 2020 presidential primaries,[45] 82 and 87 percent were matched, respectively. Among Democrats who voted in the presidential primaries in both years, the respective figures were 60 and 68 percent – higher than the estimates from self-reported turnout, but still less pronounced than Republicans. In the general election, matched Republicans have similarly dominated, composing 79 percent of Republican voters in 2016 and 84 percent in 2020. Lagging behind here too, matched Democrats composed 56 percent of Democratic voters in the 2016 general election, and 66 percent in the 2020 general election.

For all practical purposes, then, matched Republicans *are* the Republican electorate – in the general-election almost no less than in the presidential

---

[45] Because voter-validation data are based on state voter files, the CES does not report validated turnout statistics for voters in states with presidential caucuses. The relevant figures are based only on respondents in states that held presidential primaries, rather than caucuses or state party conventions. See the online appendix for more details.

Table 5 Self-reported turnout data, 1972–2020, by partisanship: proportion of matched partisans among partisans who reported voting in the presidential primaries and general election.

Proportion matched among partisan voters (self-reported) in the presidential primaries and general election, by partisanship

Year	Presidential primaries and caucuses		General election	
	Republican identifiers	Democratic identifiers	Republican identifiers	Democratic identifiers
1972	0.46	0.28	0.41	0.24
1976	0.51	0.30	0.47	0.25
1980	0.54	0.22	0.51	0.24
1984	Not available	Not available	0.50	0.29
1988	0.55	0.23	0.54	0.25
1992	0.53	0.33	0.52	0.33
1996	Not available	Not available	0.67	0.31
2000	Not available	Not available	0.59	0.29
2004	Not available	Not available	0.63	0.35
2008	0.75	0.44	0.67	0.39
2012	0.78	0.46	0.73	0.45
2016	0.77	0.54	0.70	0.50
2020	0.77	0.59	0.72	0.55

Source: ANES cumulative file (2022), partisan identifiers only. Self-reported turnout data.

in the 2016 and 2020 presidential primaries,[45] 82 and 87 percent were matched, respectively. Among Democrats who voted in the presidential primaries in both years, the respective figures were 60 and 68 percent – higher than the estimates from self-reported turnout, but still less pronounced than Republicans. In the general election, matched Republicans have similarly dominated, composing 79 percent of Republican voters in 2016 and 84 percent in 2020. Lagging behind here too, matched Democrats composed 56 percent of Democratic voters in the 2016 general election, and 66 percent in the 2020 general election.

For all practical purposes, then, matched Republicans *are* the Republican electorate – in the general-election almost no less than in the presidential

---

[45] Because voter-validation data are based on state voter files, the CES does not report validated turnout statistics for voters in states with presidential caucuses. The relevant figures are based only on respondents in states that held presidential primaries, rather than caucuses or state party conventions. See the online appendix for more details.

the partisan vote in both low and high-stimulus elections. The logic of spatial voting is strict: Parties can nominate more extreme candidates without losing the support of their moderate supporters.

2.8.2 Partisan Asymmetries Bottom-Up

On our account, framework matching is the mechanism regulating the polarization of the parties-in-the-electorate. Consistent with this claim, the proportion of Republicans and Democrats who know and share the ideological framework of their party has increased in tandem with elite polarization. Just as significant politically, however, Republicans are markedly more likely than Democrats to know and share the ideological framework of their party (Figure 8) – at every point in time. It follows straightforwardly that core Republicans will play a larger electoral role than core Democrats.

Table 5 confirms this prediction, reporting rates of matching for Republican and Democratic voters separately. The differences are dramatic. By 1976, matched Republicans composed more than half of the Republicans who self-reported voting in the presidential primaries; by 1980, they composed more than half of Republican general-election voters. By 2020, their share of the Republican electorate had skyrocketed; matched Republicans composed 72 and 77 percent of self-reported voters in the general election and presidential primaries, respectively.

In contrast, it was not until 2016, perhaps under the pressure of Donald Trump's first campaign, that matched Democrats made up a majority of Democratic identifiers in either the presidential primaries or the general election. Even then, matched Republicans' share of their party's voters was 20 percentage points higher in the general election and 23 points higher in the presidential primaries. Simply put, the Republican electorate has a larger ideological core than the Democratic electorate.

As always, caution is called for. Survey respondents often claim to have voted when they did not. The more marginal their ties to a party, it is fair to expect, the more likely they are to be false positives, falsely reporting (perhaps due to social desirability bias) that they turned out to vote. With voter-validated data from the Cooperative Congressional Election Study (CCES, now CES), we can obtain more accurate assessments of matched partisans' shares of the electorate.

Table 6 examines the proportion of matched partisans among primary and general-election voters in 2016 and 2020, both in the aggregate and broken down by partisanship. For all intents and purposes, core Republicans' dominance of the presidential primaries is complete. Among Republicans who voted

Table 6 Voter-validated data: proportion of matched partisans among partisans who voted in the presidential primaries and general election.

Proportion matched among partisan voters in the presidential primaries

Year	Partisan identifiers (pooled)	Just Republicans	Just Democrats
2016	0.70	0.82	0.60
2020	0.76	0.87	0.68

Proportion matched among partisan voters in the general election

Year	Partisan identifiers (pooled)	Just Republicans	Just Democrats
2016	0.67	0.79	0.56
2020	0.75	0.84	0.66

Source: 2016 CCES Common Content (Ansolabehere and Schaffner 2017) and 2020 CES Common Content (Schaffner, Ansolabehere, and Luks 2021). Partisan identifiers only.

primaries. Matched Democrats make up a *majority* of the Democratic electorate. American politics is now ideological politics at the grassroots as well as in the halls of Congress.

2.9 Summary of Findings

2.9.1 Circumscribed Polarization

Previous studies of polarization have suggested that polarization is centered on politically engaged citizens – whether measured in terms of political interest and participation (Abramowitz 2010, 2013), general political knowledge and educational attainment (Zingher 2022), or knowledge of elite position-taking (Carsey and Layman 2006; Layman and Carsey 2002). On most measures of political sophistication, interest in elections aside, the public's sophistication has simply not increased sharply enough to account for the intensity of contemporary American politics. Rather, as the polarization of the parties-in-government increased, *less* sophistication has been required to pick up the issue context of partisan conflict (e.g., Goggin, Henderson, and Theodoridis 2020; Zingher 2022).

Political sophistication favors learning political ideas, obviously. However, our results show that it does not do the heavy lifting in explaining the policy polarization of the electorate. The polarization of the parties-in-the-electorate is circumscribed – indeed, for all practical purposes confined to – party supporters whose ideological orientation matches their party. Republicans and Democrats who know and share the ideological orientation of their party are core supporters, moving further right and left as their party leaders do, not just on this or that issue, but programmatically. Domain sorting, not issue sorting, is the rule.

2.9.2 Asymmetrical Polarization

It has long been recognized that Republicans are markedly more likely to identify with the ideological orientation of their party than Democrats are to identify with the ideological orientation of theirs (e.g., Grossman and Hopkins 2016). Bringing into the open the full implications of this asymmetry has been one of our prime objectives. The readiness of party supporters to stand with their party depends on their sharing its ideological orientation. Just as far as more Republicans than Democrats share the ideological orientation of their party, the pressure for ideological conformity will be greater within the party on the right than the party on the left.

2.9.3 Cross-Currents

Conflict commands attention. Accordingly, studies of partisan polarization have focused on the policies the two parties most vehemently contest on social welfare, race, and cultural politics. In fact, on all three agendas, politics operates on two levels – quasi-consensual as well as contested. Even as Democrats and Republicans diverge on issues like government health insurance and the appropriate balance between social spending and cutting taxes, there is broad *bipartisan* support for maintaining or increasing spending for an array of established social services – Social Security, childcare, and crime prevention. And, notwithstanding the rip tides of cultural politics, our results highlight an across-the-board increase in support for gay rights.

2.9.4 Party Cohesion versus Policy Divergence

The dramatic focus of studies on polarization is policy divergence, Republicans moving to the right and Democrats to the left. However, the cohesion of the parties-in-the-electorate – the size of the bloc of a party's supporters who stand with their party on the issues it contests – has more strategic importance. To retain supporters while pushing its policies to the extreme, the proportion of party supporters whose ideological orientation matches their party's is what matters. Taking their views all in all, moderate conservative Republicans have no policy reason to defect to an increasingly liberal Democratic Party; moderate liberal Democrats have no policy reason to defect to an increasingly conservative Republican Party. The result: The parties-in-government can move to the ideological poles, trusting that ideologically moderate core supporters will still stand with them.

2.9.5 Polarization Lags

Polarization of the parties-in-the-electorate is envisioned, implicitly, as symmetrical, with Republicans and Democrats diverging at approximately the same rate and time, near as makes no difference. So it is for social welfare politics. Polarization, measured in terms of policy divergence, is symmetrical on the social welfare agenda, with core Republicans moving to the right and core Democrats to the left. However, polarization is asymmetrical on racial politics. In the immediate aftermath of the Civil Rights Movement, white Republicans were already lined up *en masse* in support of their party's policies on race. White liberal Democrats, in contrast, came to support their party's stance on race only recently – and even, then, only on liberal policies like government aid to Blacks rather than progressive policies like affirmative action, and principally among Democrats whose ideological orientation matched their party. *Polarization lag*, the Republican coalition polarizing early and core Democrats polarizing only in the last few years, is the signature feature of the politics of race. The positions that parties take, not just the fact that they take them, matter.

White liberal Democrats' surge of support for racial liberalism offers a still more fundamental lesson. Studies of polarization too easily read like breathless narratives of a two-player game, the parties-in-government batting the ball to the parties-in-the-electorate, the parties-in-the-electorate batting it back. The two-player framework is one vital degree of freedom short. There is good reason to be uncertain about the stimulus-event(s) galvanizing Democrats to move toward their party's position on race, still more about whether it will persist or fade. What *is* clear is that white liberal Democrats reacted to an event or set of events sufficiently powerful to push them, for the first time in the post-civil rights era, toward the Democratic Party's version of racial liberalism. The lesson is a general one: reality matters.

2.9.6 Cross-Policy Domain Constraint

Constraint, operationally defined as the ability to predict what people believe about one matter given knowledge of what they believe about another, is standardly defined at the level of issues. For us, the focus of analysis is policy domains – social welfare, race, and cultural politics. Each has tracked a distinctive trajectory as electoral politics has polarized, our results show.

But over time, for partisan identifiers who know and share their party's ideology, the ties between policy domains have tightened – increasingly approximating the low-dimensional belief systems of the politically aware and active. If conservative on one policy agenda, conservative on others; if liberal on one, liberal on others.

Agreement on this picture of mass belief systems in a polarized politics, though not unanimous, is overwhelming. But here as elsewhere, the implicit presumption is symmetry. Republicans and Democrats make connections across policy domains to the same degree, near as makes no politically consequential difference. And here as elsewhere, our theme song is that the *political dynamics of partisan polarization* – far from favoring symmetry – often turn on asymmetries. As politics polarized, core white Republicans became strikingly more likely than core Democrats to connect their positions on government job assurance and government aid to Blacks. Only in 2020 did core white Democrats show an uptick in constraint on social welfare and racial attitudes. Meanwhile, core white Democrats are now markedly more likely to hold party-consistent attitudes on government aid to Blacks and abortion. The balance of advantage changes from party to party, with gains and losses from consistency across adjacent policy domains.

2.9.7 Emotion versus Belief

Three positions on the role of affect in political polarization stand out. First, Republicans' "fear and loathing" of the Democratic Party and Democrats' "fear and loathing" of the Republican Party are the propulsive force in partisan polarization, quite apart from what either believes politically (Iyengar, Sood, and Lelkes 2012; Iyengar and Westwood 2015; see also Mason 2018). Second, what regular Republicans and Democrats feel politically depends on what they believe politically (Orr and Huber 2020; Rogowski and Sutherland 2016; Webster and Abramowitz 2017). Third, what they believe politically depends on what they feel politically (Achen and Bartels 2017; Lenz 2009, 2012; Lodge and Taber 2013).

Our controlling premise is that, as the parties-in-government polarized, accelerating numbers of regular Republicans and Democrats have become ideological partisans – on the ground, real-life conservatives and liberals in their behavior – in the choices they make on candidates, policies, and parties. For them, the distinction between belief and feeling is a distinction without a difference.[46]

---

[46] Aldrich, Bae, and Sanders (2024) have a more incisive way of making the point: "... it seems to matter less to the public that their party has become increasingly aligned on the fundamentals with their own views. Rather, what is important is that the opposition is ever more consistently on the wrong side of every important aspect of politics." (3).

2.9.8 Top-Down/Bottom-Up

To get the best point of departure, our account began with the leading account of how polarization works. According to this narrative, the parties in the electorate sort on the basis of issue positions as the parties-in-government take clearer, more divergent stands (Levendusky 2009, 2010; Zingher 2022). But, critically, short of electoral retribution, polarization is a dynamic that feeds on itself, top-down and bottom-up reciprocally. The share of the party coalitions that subscribe to their party's ideological framework ratchets up, becoming more politically consequential. Precisely because they *are* core supporters, people who know and share their party's ideology act on their beliefs more regularly. They vote. Their vote matters in general elections. It matters still more in low-stimulus elections. Our results bear on only parts of the causal chain, presidential primaries and caucuses. They do not speak directly to the last link in the chain, the readiness of core supporters to favor extreme over moderate candidates. This is just one of a number of respects in which this study is only a first step in a full-scale research program on the power of ideas in mass politics.

2.9.9 Ideological Partisans

Party identifiers who match the ideological framework of their party polarized as the parties-in-government polarized. Republicans whose ideological orientation matched their party's framework moved right, and Democrats whose ideological orientation matched their party's framework moved left. They knew what their party stood for ideologically and they stood with it, not only symbolically but operationally. As the ideological polarization of the parties-in-government has intensified, their core supporters have come to systematically back their party's positions across-the-board on social welfare, race, and cultural politics. They are ideological partisans.

So our results testify. But even after reviewing them carefully, some might counter that what we call ideological partisanship is only a façade of belief. According to this alternative narrative, core supporters are not ideological partisans voicing policy attitudes out of conviction. They do not have the intellectual capacity and motivation to have an ideologically coherent take on politics. They only give an appearance of having an ideological take on politics because they are responding to party cues (see Achen and Bartels 2017). After all, a stack of survey experiments (e.g., Barber and Pope 2019) demonstrates that when Republican and Democratic identifiers are given party or candidate-branded policy alternatives, they are much more likely to take (respectively) the conservative or liberal position.[47]

Our claim is that core Republicans and Democrats use the parties as holistic models of what goes with what and why. They have learned what their party stands for and stand with it. What is evidence of learning? Certainly not the standard "follow the leader" effect in cue-taking experiments. If party supporters only back their party's position after being told it is their party's position, this is evidence that they have *not* learned its policy pledges. They need a prompt, at the least a reminder, to connect the party they identify with to its position on a policy. But *the party's positions are never specified in the ANES policy questions on which our analysis depends.* Respondents are presented with opposing policy positions. No cue is provided even implicitly, still less explicitly, that identifies which party is pledged to which policy alternative. Our results demonstrate that even when they are not reminded what their party supports, Republicans and Democrats who match their party's ideological framework back their party's position on issue after issue – predictably, consistently, and faithfully. They have learned and internalized their party's positions; they do not need party cues to recognize what their party stands for ideologically and to stand with it.

3 Implications

The research literature on polarization balloons. But notwithstanding the normal contentiousness of the research scrum, scholars agree on an impressive number of points. Three deserve special mention. First, partisan polarization is (mainly) elite-driven, with elites broadly understood to include ideological activists and groups and allied media in addition to party officials and candidates. The Republican Party propelled itself to the right, and the Democratic Party propelled itself to the left, arguably not so far as the Republican Party did to the right (Hacker and Pierson 2010; Mann and Ornstein 2012), then again possibly so (Campbell 2016).[48] Their supporters followed their lead. Second, polarization of the parties-in-the-electorate hinges on the clarity and salience of elite differences on issues (Carsey and Layman 2006; Levendusky 2009, 2010; Zingher 2022). Third, to the extent partisan identifiers polarize in response to

---

[47] Barber and Pope (2019) provide a limiting example, demonstrating that Trump supporters (including those who identify with the GOP's conservative orientation) will take a liberal or conservative position on a policy if Trump endorses a liberal or conservative position on it.

[48] DW-NOMINATE analyses (McCarty, Poole, and Rosenthal 2016; Poole and Rosenthal 2011) support the view that the Republican Party has polarized further to the right than the Democratic Party has polarized to the left. However, other measures (e.g., W-NOMINATE) appear to be more consistent with a symmetrical polarization narrative. We are indebted to John Aldrich for calling our attention to potential discrepancies between W-NOMINATE and DW-NOMINATE. See also Campbell (2016).

elite cues, polarization is presumptively symmetrical, with both Republican and Democratic identifiers diverging at the same time and the same rate nearly enough.[49]

Though we have come to quite a different view of the dynamics of partisan polarization, so far from rejecting previous research as wrong, we have relied on it at many points, above all, on demonstrations of issue sorting. Our aim has been to extend prior studies by drawing out and drawing together their diverse theoretical implications, while minimizing the number of explanatory constructs so far as possible. What do we now know *is so* that we did not know was so? What do we now know *is not so* that we thought was so?

3.1 Domain Sorting

Polarization of the parties-in-the-electorate is presumed to be a "team" phenomenon. Republicans follow their party-in-government because they are Republicans; Democrats follow their party-in-government because they are Democrats. The claim, to be clear, is not that partisans uniformly polarize. Some are more likely to do so than others, presumably because they are more politically aware and knowledgeable and therefore are more likely to know the positions that the parties and candidates have taken (Freeder, Lenz, and Turney 2018; Layman and Carsey 2002; Levendusky 2009, 2010; Zingher 2022). But the everyday working assumption has been that their psychological identification with a party, their emotional attachment to it, motivates regular Republicans and Democrats to follow their party's lead.

Polarization so conceived is loyalty politics: Partisan identifiers mimicking the positions of their party, not because they share these convictions, but because they are emotionally bound to their party. The theoretical framework remains the landmark *The American Voter* (Campbell et al. 1960). According to Campbell et al. (1960), party identification consists of "an individual's affective orientation to an important group-objective in his environment" (121). The tip-off adjective, *affective*, signals the politically vacuous character of the attachment. No surprise, then, that scholars sympathetic to this formulation describe

---

[49] To be clear, this third conclusion tends to be presumed rather than explicitly asserted. Assuming that mass opinion polarizes in response to the behavior of elites, there is no theoretical reason why Republican and Democratic identifiers would not move in opposite directions simultaneously. Indeed, some analyses depend on an assumption of symmetric polarization. For example, Layman and Carsey (2002) use confirmatory factor analysis to quantify Democratic and Republican identifiers' positions on social welfare, cultural, and racial issues. Yet their estimation procedure assumes distinct factor scores for Democrats, Republicans, and independents, expressing Democratic and Republican identifiers' average positions in terms of the *difference* from independents' average positions.

partisans in blisteringly unflattering terms. An example: Achen and Bartels (2017) entitle a chapter "It Feels Like We're Thinking."

It is not necessary to take so deprecatory a view of ordinary citizens' reasoning about politics. A robust line of research has called out the role of signaling and issue sorting. Regular Republicans and Democrats have increasingly taken the side of their party on particular issues as a function of the clarity and salience of the differences between the parties-in-government (Fiorina 2017; Fiorina, Abrams, and Pope 2011; Levendusky 2009, 2010). An extension of the concept of issue sorting follows from our reasoning and results – domain sorting.

The debate over the role of government (how far is the government responsible for helping those who are disadvantaged? How far is it up to individuals to overcome the challenges in their lives?) has been the nerve of American electoral politics since the early New Deal period. The parties' opposing stances – government activism versus individual responsibility – have since the 1930s defined what they stand for. By the early 1970s, Republicans and Democrats in ideological sync with their party were accordingly on opposing sides on social welfare issues – and then diverged further, under the pressure of the ideological polarization of elite politics. Core Republicans have become increasingly conservative on social welfare issues, core Democrats increasingly liberal, at the same time and at the same rate as near as makes no difference.

The politics of race, however, is not simply a version of the politics of social welfare under a different name. The modern Democratic Party asks Americans to acknowledge that a historic wrong was done (and indeed, is *still* being done) to Black Americans – and therefore that exceptional efforts are imperative to put things right (see Smith and King 2024). Hence the profoundly different dynamics of white Americans' racial attitudes – asymmetrical rather than symmetrical polarization. Throughout the whole fifty-year period our data cover, white Republicans who know and share their party's ideology have overwhelmingly backed their party on issues of race. In contrast, white Democrats have historically refused to embrace the Democratic Party's progressive version of racial liberalism. Indeed, until the past two election cycles, the best that even white Democrats who know and share their party's ideological orientation could manage was to track the neutral midpoint on racial issues, not quite against, but then again not quite in support of, government efforts to promote racial equality. Polarization lag, white Republicans mobilizing early and thoroughly in support of racial conservatism, white Democrats only recently in support of racial liberalism, is the telltale marker of the over-time dynamics of racial politics.

Cultural politics is a hybrid. On abortion, Republicans have lagged Democrats. As the parties began to diverge on the issue of abortion (see

Adams 1997), core Democrats started off decidedly pro-choice and grew only more so. Core Republicans were initially pro-choice too, albeit somewhat less than their Democratic counterparts. Gradually but unremittingly, core Republicans reversed their position and migrated in favor of supporting more restrictions on abortion.

The ANES trends on attitudes toward gun control suggest that the best evidence sometimes is not good enough. On the one hand, Republicans have become much less likely to support gun control measures. On the other hand, regulations on gun control policies became weaker during the time period our data cover (2000–2020). What should we make of resistance to supporting more regulations when regulations have become laxer? Especially if they know and share the ideological orientation of their party, Democrats have backed making gun purchases more difficult. Yet Democrats' drop in support for gun control in 2008 – very much including core Democrats – underscores the limitations of available ANES measures on gun control. Yet another point where the most we can know is much less than we need to know because the best data available are not good enough.

We do have excellent data on moral traditionalism, indexed by the four-item measure that has appeared in multiple iterations of the ANES since 1986. Strictly speaking, core Republicans did not polarize on moral traditionalism. From 1986 on, they have overwhelmingly affirmed culturally conservative values. In contrast, core Democrats tracked the neutral midpoint on moral traditionalism until the mid-1990s. Only then did they begin to trend liberal, and only in recent cycles did their liberalism on moral traditionalism match core Republicans' long-standing conservatism – yet another example of polarization lag.

3.2 Constraint

Philip Converse published "The Nature of Belief Systems in Mass Publics" in 1964. The results of our analyses may appear to contradict his. The appearance of contradiction is misleading, as it is the result of neglecting the *political dynamics* of polarization.

In the most thorough defense of Converse (1964) to date, Kinder and Kalmoe (2017) comprehensively review the many facets of Converse's analysis. Ours takes account of only one, constraint. Their conclusion is that "the argument by Converse more than half a century ago requires a bit of tinkering, but little more than that" (Kinder and Kalmoe 2017, 43). Ours is that polarization has wrought dramatic changes.

Why the opposite conclusions? Kinder and Kalmoe (2017) analyzed the ANES from 1972 to 2012, the latest study available to them, concluding that the constraint of Americans' belief systems is minimal – with correlations between issue-pairs averaging 0.16 – and the rate of per-decade increase a miniscule 0.01 (Kinder and Kalmoe 2017, 28–29). In measuring constraint, Kinder and Kalmoe calculated the correlation between positions on specific issues *no matter what the policies were about* – whether defense, abortion, immigration, foreign affairs, or civil rights. The reason to do so is not obvious, at any rate to us. What reason is there to suppose that, if you know what people think about one policy, you should be able to predict what they think about any and every other conceivable policy? Our concern, in contrast, is with constraint between issues on the same policy agenda – social welfare, racial, and cultural issues – "natural wholes," to use Converse's term.

There is a deeper problem with the claim that Converse's account of the 1950s requires "only a bit of tinkering" to square with the politics of today. Analyses of constraint typically focus on the strength of the connections between positions on issues. However, the most profound feature of Converse's analysis of constraint was the virtual disconnect between the positions that voters take and the party with which they identify.[50] But that is precisely the point on which almost every study agrees that politics now is different from the politics of the 1950s. The connection between party identification and policy preferences has dramatically increased in strength. That is, after all, what everyone means when they report that the parties-in-the-electorate have polarized: Republicans now predictably, consistently line up on the right, Democrats predictably, consistently on the left, on the issues the Republican and Democratic parties contest – to a degree that was inconceivable at the high noon of the politics that Converse illuminated (Abramowitz 2010, 2013, 2015, 2018; Bafumi and Shapiro 2009; Fiorina 2017; Fiorina, Abrams, and Pope 2011; Lupton et al. 2015; Zingher 2022).

It does not follow, it should be obvious, that Converse's model of public opinion no longer applies. On the contrary, our results show that it does and makes plain why. The polarization of Republican and Democratic identifiers is centered on – indeed, for all practical purposes restricted to – Republicans and Democrats who know and share the ideological orientation of their party. In 2020, party identifiers were split, approximately half knowing and sharing the overall outlook of their party, half not. That leaves plenty of room, even in a polarized politics, for a Conversian account to apply to a large swath of the electorate.[51]

---

[50] For the domestic policy issues that Converse (1964) examined, the median tau-gamma correlation with party identification was 0.16 (Converse 1964, 228).

[51] On our scorecard, in 2020, fully matched partisans composed 53 percent of eligible voters. The other 47 percent were either partially matched partisans, unmatched partisans, or pure independents.

3.3 Party Cohesion

Polarization envisioned as policy divergence – the widening gap between the parties, Republicans to the right, Democrats to the left – has been the focus of research. Yet from the perspective of party leadership, policy cohesion – the share of the party coalition that both shares the party's ideological orientation and aligns with it on a contested issue – is more consequential. From the point of view of a party's leadership willing to risk extremes, it is not necessary that the median supporter's preferences match the median leader's preferences to retain their support. It is only necessary that their party's policies and candidates be their *spatial favorite*. In a polarized politics, a moderately conservative Republican has no policy incentive to defect to the Democratic Party – a party that, after all, is polarizing to the left. A moderately liberal Democrat has no policy incentive to defect to the Republican Party – a party that, after all, is polarizing to the right. It follows that, for the parties-in-government to retain the backing of their supporters, it is only necessary that the parties' core supporters take their party's *side* on the issues their party contests.

Yet there are limits on top-down politics. The logic of top-down polarization is not false, but it is incomplete. The positions that a party takes, not just the fact it takes them, matter. Among non-Hispanic whites, core Democrats sat on the sidelines on race throughout almost the whole of the period our data cover, while core Republicans mobilized on racial issues early and thoroughly. Why, it is only fair to ask, did the Democratic Party not get punished by core supporters?

We do not have an answer; we do have a conjecture. Claggett and Shafer (2010) demonstrate that, while the salience of other policy domains waxed and waned, social welfare attitudes had a significant effect on the presidential vote in each election from 1948 to 2004; others demonstrate that social welfare attitudes continue to be the primary policy domain structuring public opinion (Carmines, Ensley, and Wagner 2012; Feldman and Johnston 2014). Competing positions on social welfare and the size and scope of government thus define the political identities of the major parties. As the polarization of the parties-in-government becomes increasingly stark, social welfare policies are the focal point, we would wager, for Democrats who identify with the ideological orientation of their party.[52]

---

[52] In his study of political attitudes in the immediate run-up to the 2016 presidential election, Bartels (2018) suggests that Democrats are more animated by social welfare than cultural issues, while Republicans demonstrate the reverse pattern. Note that in Bartels' factor analysis, racial attitudes load primarily onto the latent dimension representing cultural conservatism, rather than limited government conservatism.

3.4 Political Convictions: Amalgams of Beliefs and Emotions

The idea that the political polarization of the electorate is primarily a matter of affect – of emotion and not belief, above all of hostility and suspicion, in the telling phrase "fear and loathing" – of the members of one party toward the other has wide currency. Understandably, a polarized politics is a politics of strong feelings. But to bring into the open the political dynamics of polarization, it is necessary to ask whether (and for whom) polarization is only or mainly or substantially a matter of strong feelings.

Here is a thought experiment.[53] You know what your party stands for and you stand with it. You know that the other party opposes what you and your party support. You know – no elaborate reasoning required here – that if the opposing party wins the election, what you believe needs to be done will not be done, still worse, what needs not to be done will be done. How will you react if your party loses and the other party wins? How likely is your reaction to be, ho-hum?

This thought experiment, fortunately, has an empirical answer.[54] It is not necessary to be in ideological sync with your party to dislike the opposing party. But for Republicans and Democrats who know and believe in what their party stands for, what they believe in and how they feel about the party that opposes what they believe inextricably fuse. For them, the distinction between their political convictions and their fear and loathing of the other party is, empirically, a distinction without a difference.

3.5 Ideological Politics as Spatial Politics

Ideology, Converse (1964) proclaimed, is a hierarchical "cognitive structure, capped by superordinate values or postures toward man and society" (211). Ideological reasoning, so viewed, is deductive – an inference from abstract principle to middle-range principle, then inference from middle-range principle to specific policy preference – all of this step-by-step, an antiseptically logical chain of reasoning. The classic studies of public opinion taught the same lesson: Ordinary citizens' interest in politics is erratic; their knowledge of politics and public affairs superficial; and their grasp of political ideas and abstractions still more so. Like night follows day, it followed that ideology was outside the reach of the wider public.

---

[53] In a major advance, Druckman et al. (2024) demonstrate the force of hostility towards the other party in responding to its positions.

[54] See Aldrich, Bae, and Sanders (2024, ch. 6) for a more thoroughly elaborated answer to this thought experiment. The authors see polarization not as policy extremism, but as a single reinforced cleavage, consistency across policies and policy domains.

Our controlling premise is the rejection of this portrait of ideological reasoning as inside-out. Ordinary citizens do not use ideological categories to organize and order their political ideas, à la William James' trope of newborns organizing "the blooming, buzzing confusion" of sensory impressions. They – we – do not impose our organizing scheme on political ideas, candidates, and parties. How they are organized and ordered in the world *is* our starting point.

Ideological politics *is* spatial politics, the positions and policies of the Republican and Democratic parties codified into policy domains, each ordered on a dimension running from left to right. To use political parties as holistic models of "what goes with what," people must be looking in the right direction – Republicans orienting themselves as conservatives and Democrats orienting themselves as liberals are looking in the right direction; those who do not are looking in the wrong direction. The dynamics of partisan polarization follow. The sharper the contrast between the programmatic differences between the Republican and Democratic parties, the easier it is for their supporters to match the spatial orientation of their party and to stand with it programmatically, Republicans systematically lining up on the right and Democrats on the left. In turn, the more programmatically cohesive the parties' supporters, the more latitude their party's leaders have to push their policies toward the poles.

Little is gained by arguing about words. Similarity of spatial orientation is key. Republicans who know they are conservative and that theirs is the conservative party, who line up predictably, systematically on the right, are ideological partisans. The same can be said for Democrats who know that they are liberals and that theirs is the liberal party, who line up predictably and systematically on the left. American politics now *is* ideological politics, not just for political activists and public intellectuals, but also for a politically consequential portion of the wider public.

Similarity of spatial orientation is also the key to the ideological skew of the party system. As elite politics polarized, the proportion of ideological partisans in both parties increased too. However, from the start of the approximately fifty-year time span our study covers, the proportion of ideological partisans in the Republican coalition has been decisively larger than the proportion of ideological partisans in the Democratic coalition, *at every point in time*. By way of calibration, in 2020, on the order of seven out of ten Republicans both knew and shared their party's ideology, compared to just over half of Democrats. Compared to the Democratic Party, then, the Republican Party has a far larger share of supporters ideologically in sync with it, ready to take their party's side even when the party's leaders push their policies to the limit. Just so far as the Republican Party is ideologically more cohesive than the Democratic Party, an ideological skew is wired into the party system.

3.6 The Heterogeneity of Party Identification

Party identification has been conceptualized in multiple ways – as an emotional attachment (Campbell et al., 1960), a social identity (Green, Schickler, and Palmquist 2002), and an expressive identity (Huddy, Mason, and Aarøe 2015), among others.[55] However, regardless of how it has been conceptualized, homogeneity of meaning has been the presumption. Whatever party identification means, it means the same thing for all party identifiers (but see Arceneaux and Vander Wielen 2017; Elliot 2023).

Our approach stands or falls on one claim: *Party identification now means one thing to some party identifiers and something quite different to many others.* For some, consistent with the canonical conception of party identification, attachment to a party flags an emotional bond and not much more. But for accelerating numbers of Republicans and Democrats, their bond with their party is substantive as well as emotional. For them, a good part of what it means to be a Republican is to be a conservative; a good part of what it means to be a Democrat is to be a liberal.

The heterogeneity of party identification is the key to the dynamics of the polarization of the parties-in-the-electorate. Partisan polarization is circumscribed, confined to Republicans and Democrats whose ideological orientation matches their party's. Lumping ideological and traditional partisans together, presuming that what it means to identify with a political party means the same thing for both, conceals what is driving American politics now – an upsurge of regular Republicans and Democrats who know what their party stands for and stand with it.

3.7 A Last Word

Studies of democratic backsliding are piling up. The root idea is that the risk is looming large because citizens are failing to enforce democratic norms and political leaders are not being sanctioned for anti-democratic initiatives (e.g., Clayton 2024; Graham and Svolik 2020; Simonovits, McCoy, and Littvay 2022). An increasingly polarized electorate is said to be part of the story, an upswelling of populism another part, partisan hypocrisy still another part, and a superficial understanding (and misunderstanding) of the idea of democracy yet another.

It never pays to underestimate ignorance and intemperateness. Our results, however, have brought into the open a threat from a quite different direction. Democrats and Republicans who know what their party stands for and stand

---

[55] See especially Dennis' (1988a, 1988b, 1992) innovative studies of political independents.

with it are a textbook model of democratic citizenship. Their outlook on politics is ideologically consistent but modally moderate. Hence the irony: in a polarized politics, the driving force is not an irrational craving of their supporters for an extreme, intemperate politics. It is instead that the parties-in-government are freed up to push policies to the limit just so far as their core supporters are making the rational choice, given the alternatives on offer.

References

Abramowitz, A. I. (2010). *The Disappearing Center: Engaged Citizens, Polarization, and American Democracy*. New Haven, CT: Yale University Press.

Abramowitz, A. I. (2013). *The Polarized Public: Why American Government is So Dysfunctional*. New York: Pearson Longman.

Abramowitz, A. I. (2015). The new American electorate: Partisan, sorted, and polarized. In J. A. Thurber & A. Yoshinaka, eds., *American Gridlock*. New York: Cambridge University Press, pp. 19–44.

Abramowitz, A. I. (2018). *The Great Alignment: Race, Party Transformation, and the Rise of Donald Trump*. New Haven, CT: Yale University Press.

Abramowitz, A. I. & Saunders, K. L. (1998). Ideological realignment in the U.S. electorate. *Journal of Politics* 60(3): 634–652.

Abramowitz, A. I. & Saunders, K. L. (2006). Exploring the bases of partisanship in the American electorate: Social identity vs. ideology. *Political Research Quarterly* 59(2): 175–187.

Abramowitz, A. I. & Saunders, K. L. (2008). Is polarization a myth? *Journal of Politics* 70(2): 542–555.

Achen, C. H. (1975). Mass political attitudes and the survey response. *American Political Science Review* 69: 1218–1231.

Achen, C. H. & Bartels, L. M. (2017). *Democracy for Realists*. Princeton, NJ: Princeton University Press.

Aldrich, J. H., Bae, S., & Sanders, B. K. (2024). *The Fundamental Voter: American Electoral Democracy, 1952–2020*. New York: Oxford University Press.

Allamong, M. B., Beutel, B., Jeong, J., & Kellstedt, P. M. (N.d.). Open-ended survey responses and political conceptualizations in a polarized era. Unpublished working paper.

Adams, G. D. (1997). Abortion: Evidence of an issue evolution. *American Journal of Political Science* 41(3): 718–737.

American National Election Studies. (1999). ANES 1988 time series study full release [dataset and documentation]. May 21, 1999 version. https://electionstudies.org/data-center/1988-time-series/.

American National Election Studies. (2021). ANES 2020 time series study full release [dataset and documentation]. February 10, 2022 version. https://electionstudies.org/data-center/2020-time-series-study/.

References

American National Election Studies. (2022). Time series cumulative data file (1948–2020) [dataset and documentation]. September 16, 2022 version. https://electionstudies.org/data-center/anes-time-series-cumulative-data-file/.

Ansolabehere, S., Rodden. J., & Snyder, J. M. (2008). The strength of issues: Using multiple measures to gauge preference stability, ideological constraint, and issue voting. *American Political Science Review* 102(2): 215–232.

Ansolabehere, S. & Schaffner, B. F. (2017). CCES common content, 2016. https://doi.org/10.7910/DVN/GDF6Z0, Harvard Dataverse, V4, UNF:6: WhtR8dNtMzReHC295hA4cg== [fileUNF].

Arceneaux, K. & Vander Wielen, R. J. (2017). *Taming Intuition*. Cambridge: Cambridge University Press.

Atkinson, M. L., Coggins, K. E., Stimson, J. A., & Baumgartner, F. R. (2021). *The Dynamics of Public Opinion*. New York: Cambridge University Press.

Bafumi, J. & Shapiro, R. Y. (2009). A new partisan voter. *Journal of Politics* 71(1): 1–24.

Bandura, A. (1986). *Social Foundations of Thought and Action*. Englewood Heights, NJ: Prentice-Hall.

Bandura, A. (2023). *Social Cognitive Theory*. New York: Wiley.

Barber, M. & Pope, J. C. (2018). Who is ideological? Measuring ideological consistency in the American public. *The Forum* 16(1): 97–122.

Barber, M. & Pope, J. C. (2019). Does party trump ideology? Disentangling party and ideology in America. *American Political Science Review* 113(1): 38–54.

Bartels, L. M. (2018). Partisanship in the Trump era. *Journal of Politics* 80(4): 1483–1494.

Broockman, D. (2016). Approaches to studying policy representation. *Legislative Studies Quarterly* 41(1): 181–215.

Campbell, A. P., Converse, P. E., Miller, W. E., & Stokes, D. E. (1960). *The American Voter*. New York: John Wiley and Sons.

Campbell, J. E. (2016). *Polarized: Making Sense of a Divided America*. Princeton, NJ: Princeton University Press.

Carmines, E. G., Ensley, M. J., & Wagner, M. W. (2012). Who fits the left-right divide? Partisan polarization in the American electorate. *American Behavioral Scientist* 56(12): 1631–1653.

Carmines, E. G. & Stimson, J. A. (1989). *Issue Evolution: Race and the Transformation of American Politics*. Princeton, NJ: Princeton University Press.

Carsey, T. M. & Layman, G. C. (2006). Changing sides or changing minds? Party identification and policy preferences in the American electorate. *American Journal of Political Science* 50(2): 464–477.

References

Claggett, W. J. M. & Shafer, B. E. (2010). *The American Public Mind: The Issues Structure of Mass Politics in the Postwar United States*. New York: Cambridge University Press.

Clayton, K. (2024). *The Public's Response to Incremental Democratic Backsliding and Effective Solutions*. PhD dissertation, Stanford University.

Converse, P. E. (1964). The nature of belief systems in mass publics. In D. Apter, ed., *Ideology and Discontent*. New York: Free Press, pp. 206–261.

Costa, M. (2021). Ideology, not affect: What Americans want from political representation. *American Journal of Political Science* 65(2): 342–358.

Dennis, J. (1988a). Political independence in America, part I: On being an independent partisan supporter. *British Journal of Political Science* 18: 77–109.

Dennis, J. (1988b). Political independence in America, part II: Towards a theory. *British Journal of Political Science* 14: 197–219.

Dennis, J. (1992). Political independence in America, part II: In search of closet partisans. *Political Behavior* 14: 197–219.

Dias, N. & Lelkes, Y. (2022). The nature of affective polarization: Disentangling policy disagreement from partisan identity. *American Journal of Political Science* 66(3): 775–790.

Diermeier, D. & Li, C. (2019). Partisan affect and elite polarization. *American Political Science Review* 113(1): 277–281.

Downs, A. (1957). *An Economic Theory of Democracy*. New York: Harper and Row.

Druckman, J. N., Klar, S., Krupnikov, Y., Levendusky, M., & Ryan, J. B. (2024). *Partisan Hostility and American Democracy*. Chicago, IL: University of Chicago Press.

Elder, E. M. & O'Brian, N. (2022). Social groups as the source of political belief systems: Fresh evidence on an old theory. *American Political Science Review* 116(4): 1407–1424.

Ellis, C. & Stimson, J. A. (2012). *Ideology in America*. New York: Cambridge University Press.

Elliott, K. J. (2024). What is it like to be a partisan? Measures of partisanship and its value for democracy. *Perspectives on Politics* 22(3): 584–598.

Erikson, R. S., MacKuen, M. B., Stimson, J. A. (2002). *The Macro Polity*. New York: Cambridge University Press.

Feldman, S. & Johnston, C. (2014). Understanding the determinants of political ideology: Implications of structural complexity. *Political Psychology* 35(3): 337–358.

Fiorina, M. P. (2017). *Unstable Majorities*. Stanford, CA: Hoover Institution Press.

Fiorina, M. P., Abrams, S. J., & Pope, J. C. (2011). *Culture War? The Myth of a Polarized America*. New York: Pearson Longman Press.

Fowler, A., Hill, S. J., Lewis, J. B., et al. (2023). Moderates. *American Political Science Review* 117: 643–660.

Fowler, A., Huber, G. A., Jin, R., & Orr, L. V. (N.d.) Why are you a Democrat? Studying the origins of party identification and partisan animosity with open-ended survey questions. Unpublished working paper.

Freeder, S., Lenz, G. S., & Turney, S. (2018). The importance of knowing 'what goes with what': Reinterpreting the evidence on policy attitude stability. *Journal of Politics* 81(1): 274–290.

Gärdenfors, P. (2020). Can we use conceptual spaces to model moral principles? *Review of Philosophy and Psychology* 12: 373–395.

Gärdenfors, P. (2000). *Conceptual Spaces: The Geometry of Thought*. Cambridge, MA: MIT Press.

Gilens, M. (1999). *Why Americans Hate Welfare: Race, Media, and the Politics of Antipoverty Policy*. Chicago, IL: University of Chicago Press.

Goggin, S. N., Henderson, J. A., & Theodoridis, A. G. (2020). What goes with red and blue? Mapping partisan and ideological associations in the minds of voters. *Political Behavior* 42: 985–1013.

Goren, P. (2005). Party identification and core political values. *American Journal of Political Science* 49(4): 881–896.

Goren, P. (2013). *On Voter Competence*. New York: Oxford University Press.

Goren, P., Federico, C. M., & Kittilson, M. C. (2009). Source cues, partisan identities, and political value expression. *American Journal of Political Science* 53(4): 805–820.

Graham, M. H. & Svolik, M. W. (2020). Democracy in America? Partisanship, polarization, and the robustness of support for democracy in the United States. *American Political Science Review* 114(2): 392–409.

Green, D., Palmquist, B., &. Schickler, E. (2002). *Partisan Hearts and Minds*. New Haven, CT: Yale University Press.

Grossman, M. & Hopkins, D. (2016). *Asymmetric Politics: Ideological Republicans and Group Interest Democrats*. New York: Oxford University Press.

Hacker, J. & Pierson, P. (2010). *Winner-Take-All Politics: How Washington Made the Rich Richer and Turned its Back on the Middle Class*. New York: Simon and Schuster.

Hare, C. (2022). Constrained citizens? Ideological structure and conflict extension in the U.S. electorate, 1980-2016. *British Journal of Political Science* 52(4): 1602–1621.

Hare, C., Highton, B., & Jones, B. (2024). Assessing the structure of policy preferences: A hard test of the low-dimensionality hypothesis. *Journal of Politics* 86(2): 672–686.

Hersh, E. (2020). *Politics is for Power*. New York: Scribner.

Hetherington, M. J. (2009). Putting polarization in perspective. *British Journal of Political Science* 39(2): 413–448.

Hill, S. J. & Tausanovitch, C. (2017). Southern realignment, party sorting, and the polarization of American primary electorates, 1958–2012. *Public Choice* 176: 107–132.

Hopkins, D. J. (2023). *Stable Condition: Elites' Limited Influence on Health Care Attitudes*. New York: Russell Sage Foundation.

Huddy, L., Mason, L., & Aarøe, L. (2015). Expressive partisanship: Campaign involvement, political emotion, and partisan identity. *American Political Science Review* 109(1): 1–17.

Iyengar, S., Sood, G., & Lelkes, Y. (2012). Affect, not ideology: A social identity perspective on polarization. *Public Opinion Quarterly* 76(3): 405–431.

Iyengar, S. & Krupenkin, M. (2018). The strengthening of partisan affect. *Political Psychology* 39: 201–218.

Iyengar, S. & Westwood, S. (2015). Fear and loathing across party lines: New evidence for group polarization. *American Journal of Political Science* 59(3): 690–707.

Kabaservice, G. (2012). *Rule and Ruin: The Downfall of Moderation and the Destruction of the Republican Party, from Eisenhower to the Tea Party*. New York: Oxford University Press.

Katznelson, I. (2014). *Fear Itself: The New Deal and the Origins of Our Time*. New York: W. W. Norton.

Keith, B. E., Magleby, D. B., Nelson, C. J., Orr, E. A., & Westlye, M. C. (1992). *The Myth of the Independent Voter*. Berkeley, CA: University of California Press.

Kinder, D. R. & Kalmoe, N. P. (2017). *Neither Liberal nor Conservative: Ideological Innocence in the American Public*. Chicago, IL: University of Chicago Press.

Klar, S. & Krupnikov, Y. (2016). *Independent Politics*. New York: Cambridge University Press.

Kozlowski, A. C. & Murphy, J. P. (2021). Issue alignment and partisanship in the American public: Revisiting the "partisans without constraint" thesis. *Social Science Research* 94: 102948.

Layman, G. C. (2001). *The Great Divide: Religious and Cultural Conflict in American Party Politics*. New York: Columbia University Press.

Layman, G. C. & Carsey, T. M. (2002). Party polarization and conflict extension in the American electorate. *American Journal of Political Science* 46(4): 786–802.

Leege, D. C., Wald, K. D., Krueger, B. S., & Mueller, P. D. (2002). *The Politics of Cultural Differences: Social Change and Voter Mobilization Strategies in the Post-New Deal Period*. Princeton, NJ: Princeton University Press.

Lenz, G. S. (2009). Learning and opinion change, not priming: Reconsidering the priming hypothesis. *American Journal of Political Science* 53(4): 821–837.

Lenz, G. S. (2012). *Follow the Leader? How Voters Respond to Politicians' Policies and Performance*. Chicago, IL: University of Chicago Press.

Levendusky, M. S. (2009). *The Partisan Sort*. Chicago, IL: University of Chicago Press.

Levendusky, M. S. (2010). Clearer cues, more consistent voters: A benefit of elite polarization. *Political Behavior* 32(1): 111–131.

Lewis, A. (2017). *The Rights Turn in Conservative Christian Politics: How Abortion Transformed the Culture Wars*. New York: Cambridge University Press.

Lodge, M. & Taber, C. S. (2013). *The Rationalizing Voter*. New York: Cambridge University Press.

Long, J. A. (2022). *jtools: Analysis and Presentation of Social Scientific Data*. R package version 2.2.0, https://cran.r-project.org/package=jtools.

Luker, K. (1985). *Abortion and the Politics of Motherhood*. Berkeley, CA: University of California Press.

Lupton, R. N., Myers, W. M., & Thornton, J. R. (2015). Political sophistication and the dimensionality of elite and mass attitudes, 1980–2004. *Journal of Politics* 77(2): 368–380.

Mann, T. & Ornstein, N. (2012). *It's Even Worse than It Looks*. New York: Basic Books.

Mansbridge, J. (1986). *Why We Lost the ERA*. New York: Cambridge University Press.

Mason, L. (2014). "I disrespectfully agree": The differential effects of partisan sorting on social and issue polarization. *American Journal of Political Science* 59(1): 126–145.

Mason, L. (2018). *Uncivil Agreement: How Politics Became Our Identity.* Chicago, IL: University of Chicago Press.

Mason, L. & Wronski, J. (2018). One tribe to bind them all: How our social group attachments strengthen partisanship. *Political Psychology* 39: 257–277.

McCarty, N., Poole, K. T., & Rosenthal, H. M. (2016). *Polarized America: The Dance of Ideology and Unequal Riches* (2nd ed.) Cambridge, MA: MIT Press.

Noel, H. (2013). *Political Ideologies and Political Parties in America.* New York: Cambridge University Press.

Olapido, G. (2021). Minneapolis voters reject bid to replace police with public safety department. *The Guardian*, November 3.

Orr, L. V., Fowler, A., & Huber, G. A. (2023). Is affective polarization driven by identity, loyalty or substance? *American Journal of Political Science* 67(4): 948–962.

Orr, L. V. & Huber, G. A. (2020). The policy basis of measured partisan animosity in the United States. *American Journal of Political Science* 64(3): 569–586.

Parker, K. & Hurst, K. (2021). Growing share of americans say they want more spending on police in their area. www.pewresearch.org/short-read/2021/10/26/growing-share-of-americans-say-they-want-more-spending-on-police-in-their-area/.

Pierson, P. & Schickler, E. (2020). Madison's Constitution under stress: A developmental analysis of political polarization. *Annual Review of Political Science* 16: 101–127.

Pierson, P. & Schickler, E. (2024). *Partisan Nation: The Dangerous New Logic of American Politics in a Nationalized Era.* Chicago, IL: University of Chicago Press.

Poole, K. T. & Rosenthal, H. (2011). *Ideology and Congress* (2nd ed.). New Brunswick, NJ: Transaction.

R Development Core Team. (2008). *R: A Language and Environment for Statistical Computing.* Vienna, Austria: R Foundation for Statistical Computing. ISBM 3-900051-07-0, www.R-project.org.

Rae, N. C. (1989). *The Decline and Fall of the Liberal Republicans.* New York: Oxford University Press.

Rogowski, J. C. & Sutherland, J. L. (2016). How ideology fuels affective polarization. *Political Behavior* 38(2): 485–508.

Schier, S. E. & Eberly, T. (2016). *Polarized: The Rise of Ideology in American Politics.* Lanham, MD: Rowman and Littlefield.

Shafer, B. E. & Claggett, W. J. M. (1995). *The Two Majorities: The Issue Context of Modern American Politics*. Baltimore, MD: Johns Hopkins University Press.

Simonovits, G., McCoy, J., & Littvvay, L. (2022). Democratic hypocrisy and out-group threat: Explaining citizen support for democratic erosion. *Journal of Politics* 84(3): 1806–1811.

Smith, R. M. & King, D. (2024). *America's New Racial Battle Lines*. Chicago, IL: University of Chicago Press.

Sniderman, P. S. & Carmines, E. G. (1997). *Reaching Beyond Race*. Cambridge, MA: Harvard University Press.

Sniderman, P. M., Brody, R. A, & Tetlock, P. C. (1991). *Reasoning and Choice: Explorations in Political Psychology*. New York: Cambridge University Press.

Sniderman, P. M. & Stiglitz, E. H. (2012). *The Reputational Premium: A Theory of Party Identification and Policy Reasoning*. Princeton, NJ: Princeton University Press.

Schaffner, B., Ansolabehere, S., & Luks, S. (2021). Cooperative election study common content, 2020. https://doi.org/10.7910/DVN/E9N6PH, Harvard Dataverse, V4, UNF:6:zWLoanzs2F3awt+875kWBg== [fileUNF].

Tesler, M. (2016). *Post-Racial or Most-Racial? Race and Politics in the Obama Era*. Chicago, IL: University of Chicago Press.

Valentino, N. & Sears, D. O. (2005). Old times there are not forgotten: Race and partisan realignment in the contemporary South. *American Journal of Political Science* 49(3): 672–688.

Wattenburg, M. (2019). The changing nature of mass belief systems: The rise of concept and policy ideologues. *Critical Review* 31(2): 198–229.

Webster, S. W. & Abramowitz, A. I. (2017). The ideological foundations of affective polarization in the U.S. electorate. *American Politics Research* 45(4): 621–647.

Wickham, H. (2016). *ggplot2: Elegant Graphics for Data Analysis*. New York: Springer-Verlag. ISBN 978-3-319-24277-4, https://ggplot2.tidyverse.org.

Zaller, J. R. (1992). *The Nature and Origins of Mass Opinion*. New York: Cambridge University Press.

Zingher, J. N. (2022). *Political Choice in a Polarized America*. New York: Oxford University Press.

Data Availability Statement

All data and code required to reproduce the results and figures in this Element are available at https://dataverse.harvard.edu/dataset.xhtml?persistentId=doi:10.7910/DVN/3SYLLO. Please direct questions to Eric R. Schmidt (corresponding author) at schmier@millsaps.edu.

Acknowledgments

Many have helped, many of them more than once: John Aldrich, Paul Allen Beck, Christopher DeSante, Jamie Druckman, Drew Englehardt, Morris Fiorina, Christopher Hare, Benjamin Highton, Seth Hill, Daniel Hopkins, Gregory Huber, Geoffrey Layman, Yphtach Lelkes, Eric Schickler, Steven Webster, and L.J. Zigerell. Series editor, Frances Lee, gave us a warm welcome and resolute backing, and two anonymous reviewers gave encouragement and insightful criticisms. Schmidt extends thanks to Victoria Gorham, Kurt Thaw, Tim Ward, Stephanie Rolph, Keith Dunn, and Frank Neville at Millsaps College for their invaluable early-career support, and to Ted Carmines and Paul Sniderman for their mentorship and confidence. Carmines expresses his appreciation to the Warner O. Chapman Professorship that provided time and resources to support this research. Sniderman, yet again, is indebted to Stephen Haber, Jackie Sargent, and Eliana Vasquez at Stanford for support of all forms and to Thomas Piazza, always a partner and my model of a life well lived.

To the memory of Thomas Piazza.

Cambridge Elements

American Politics

Frances E. Lee
Princeton University

Frances E. Lee is Professor of Politics at the Woodrow Wilson School of Princeton University. She is author of *Insecure Majorities: Congress and the Perpetual Campaign* (2016), *Beyond Ideology: Politics, Principles and Partisanship in the U.S. Senate* (2009), and coauthor of *Sizing Up the Senate: The Unequal Consequences of Equal Representation* (1999).

Advisory Board
Larry M. Bartels, *Vanderbilt University*
Marc Hetherington, *University of North Carolina at Chapel Hill*
Geoffrey C. Layman, *University of Notre Dame*
Suzanne Mettler, *Cornell University*
Hans Noel, *Georgetown University*
Eric Schickler, *University of California, Berkeley*
John Sides, *George Washington University*
Laura Stoker, *University of California, Berkeley*

About the Series
The Cambridge Elements Series in American Politics publishes authoritative contributions on American politics. Emphasizing works that address big, topical questions within the American political landscape, the series is open to all branches of the subfield and actively welcomes works that bridge subject domains. It publishes both original new research on topics likely to be of interest to a broad audience and state-of-the-art synthesis and reconsideration pieces that address salient questions and incorporate new data and cases to inform arguments.

Cambridge Elements

American Politics

Elements in the Series

The Acceptance and Expression of Prejudice During the Trump Era
Brian F. Schaffner

American Affective Polarization in Comparative Perspective
Noam Gidron, James Adams and Will Horne

The Study of US State Policy Diffusion: What Hath Walker Wrought?
Christopher Z. Mooney

Why Bad Policies Spread (and Good Ones Don't)
Charles R. Shipan and Craig Volden

The Partisan Next Door: Stereotypes of Party Supporters and Consequences for Polarization in America
Ethan C. Busby, Adam J. Howat, Jacob E. Rothschild and Richard M. Shafranek

The Dynamics of Public Opinion
Mary Layton Atkinson, K. Elizabeth Coggins, James A. Stimson and Frank R. Baumgartner

The Origins and Consequences of Congressional Party Election Agendas
Scott R. Meinke

The Full Armor of God: The Mobilization of Christian Nationalism in American Politics
Paul A. Djupe, Andrew R. Lewis and Anand E. Sokhey

The Dimensions and Implications of the Public's Reactions to the January 6, 2021, Invasion of the U.S. Capitol
Gary C. Jacobson

Cooperating Factions: A Network Analysis of Party Divisions in U.S Presidential Nominations
Rachel M. Blum, Hans C. Noel

The Haves and Have-Nots in Supreme Court Representation and Participation, 2016 to 2021
Kirsten Widner and Anna Gunderson

The Political Dynamics of Partisan Polarization
Eric R. Schmidt, Edward G. Carmines and Paul M. Sniderman

A full series listing is available at: www.cambridge.org/EAMP

For EU product safety concerns, contact us at Calle de José Abascal, 56–1º, 28003 Madrid, Spain or eugpsr@cambridge.org.

www.ingramcontent.com/pod-product-compliance
Ingram Content Group UK Ltd.
Pitfield, Milton Keynes, MK11 3LW, UK
UKHW022019160325
456332UK00005B/16